Introduction to Counselling Skills and Theory

Linda was born in Easington Colliery, Co Durham in 1958, and then moved to Leicester in the early 1960's, which is where she spent her childhood. But, it was in 'Shakespeare County,' Warwickshire, where she says she 'grew up' during and after completing her counselling diploma.

She is now an experienced counsellor, supervisor, & trainer, behavioral family therapist & author of four self help books, a children's book and four novels she has three grown up children and eight grandchildren.

Introduction to Counselling Skills and Theory

Copyright © 2014 Linda Mather

This book contains material under International and Federal Copyright Laws and Treaties. Any unauthorised reprint or use of this material is prohibited. No part of this book may be reproduced or transmitted in any form or by any means, electronic or mechanical, including photocopying, recording or by any information storage or retrieval system without express written permission from the author.

www.linda.mather.co.uk

ISBN-13 978-1489591791
ISBN-10: 1489591796

Cover art by Dreamstime

Introduction to Counselling Skills and Theory

Linda Mather

Introduction to Counselling Skills and Theory

Content

1. What to expect as part of your course.
2. What is counselling
3. Body Language & Communication
4. Listening Skills
5. Personal development tool – mental health
6. Carl Rogers core conditions
7. Reflection, Clarifying, paraphrasing and summarising and the use of silence
8. Assessments, contracting & boundaries
9. Open and closed questions
10. Personal development tool – Giving & receiving feedback Johari's window
11. Hunches & Immediacy
12. Ambivalence
13. Self disclosure
14. Helping versus enabling
15. Personal development tool - Oppression/prejudice
16. Advanced empathy (frame of reference)

Introduction to Counselling Skills and Theory

17. Listening to & exploring the feeling content & Identifying themes.
18. Different perspectives
19. Confrontation and Challenge
20. Personal development tool – The container
21. Egan's three stage model & Goal setting
22. Maslow's Hierarchy of needs.
23. Your own personal style, reflective practice & competency model
24. Taped assignment and critical evaluations
25. Personal development tool – Nurturing self
26. Confidentiality & Codes of ethics
27. Supervision & working safely
28. Research assignment
29. Transference and counter transference
30. Personal development tool – Self esteem
31. Different approaches to therapy
32. Cognitive Behavioural Therapy
33. Person Centred Therapy
34. Transactional Analysis
35. Personal development tool – Ego gram
36. Psychodynamic Therapy
37. Issues that may be brought to counselling & referrals
38. Endings

Introduction to Counselling Skills and Theory

Introduction

This book is a learning tool for students who are studying both stage one and stage two counselling theory & skills training. It is also a good resource/reference book for those doing counselling psychology courses or indeed anyone that works in public services and wishes to advance their people skills. These are the skills usually taught on an introduction to counselling and on a certificate in counselling skills.

The book is by no means designed to replace this important training, but is intended to support your learning. Counselling training not only focuses on theory, it has a huge focus on practical skills and personal development, which are equally as important as the theory.

Introduction to Counselling Skills and Theory

The format of the book is an introduction to each new skill, its meaning and how you may use it. At the end of this there might be some practical guidance on how you might practice these skills both in your personal and professional life, or some thoughts that you may like to process in your learning journal.

I will also introduce some personal development exercises, to start you on your journey of personal and professional growth.

When discussing the roles I will be using the term counsellor and client or therapist and client. However in counselling training until you reach diploma level students will usually be referred to as helper and helpee rather than counsellor/therapist and client.

I use my own teaching style through the book to make it as easy reading as possible and I have left plenty of spaces for you to write your own personal notes, which you may want to discuss with your colleagues or your tutor. Although theory and theoretical models is an element of the training I have tried to make it as understandable as I can, I hope that I have achieved this.

My experience lies within my practice as a therapist, clinical supervisor, trainer and author. When in training myself I found that there were very few easy reading therapy training books. I said that one day I would write

Introduction to Counselling Skills and Theory

one. This is that book. I followed my dream as we should all follow our dreams.

This book is a dedication to all my clients, colleagues and students who have out of awareness helped me on my journey.

Thank you.

Introduction to Counselling Skills and Theory

Chapter 1
What to expect as part of your course

It can be quite a daunting experience attending a new course at college, or university. Meeting new people, not knowing what to expect and what the expectations are of you. This can create lots of mixed feelings including excitement, fear or anxiety. Preparing yourself for a counselling course is no different.

This chapter has been written to prepare you for the difference between counselling training courses and other academic training, the expectations of you the student, and the content and the process when embarking on a counselling introduction and certificate course.

You will notice right from the moment that you walk into the classroom of a counselling programme that it is not the same as other academic courses. Counselling studies does not just focus on theory and skills; it also focuses on

Introduction to Counselling Skills and Theory

your own personal development and the engagement of the group of students also embarking on the course.

Meeting, Seating and Greeting:

The first thing that you will become aware of when entering the classroom is that unlike other courses where you may be sat behind a desk, the chairs will be set out in a semi circle with the tutor or tutors included within this circle. It is reminiscent of what a therapy group might look like. This is not because you are joining a therapy group but because counselling training mirrors the counselling process.

Tables or desks in between the client and the counsellor are seen as a barrier to the client's engagement and given that you will be engaging in a learning relationship with your colleagues and your tutor then it is just as important that the seating and greeting is welcoming from the start, with no barriers between you and the tutors or you and the other students.

Check in:

The next thing that you will be invited to do, although maybe not on the first session is 'check in'. This is when each member of the group is invited to say something about them self and about how they are feeling.

Introduction to Counselling Skills and Theory

Again it is important to remember that this is not a therapy group and not an invitation to talk about contentious issues. It is an invitation to talk about how you are feeling in the 'here and now,' or indeed what is going on in the here and now in your life. It is a mirroring of the therapeutic relationship in the same way that we would invite a client to talk to us about how they are feeling.

This can of course be quite frightening at first just as it may be frightening perhaps for the client when s/he first meets with a counsellor. However, as the relationships within the group develop talking personally about your self does get easier. Likewise as your relationship develops within the client/counsellor relationship the client finds it easier to talk about more personal issues. This emphasises the importance of the 'relationship' within any setting, particularly the counselling setting.

Journal writing:

One of the things that your tutor may ask you to do from day one of the course is to write a learning journal.

This is in a sense a sort of diary of your learning and experiences during the training. You will be invited to record not only your learning from each lesson but also the impact that this learning has had on you and your relationships. Also how this learning is facilitating growth in your own personal and professional life. It is to help

Introduction to Counselling Skills and Theory

you to explore how the training is helping with your academic and emotional growth.

This is a very important part of your learning. It will assist your own personal and professional development. It will be a huge part of the assessment of your learning and the marks towards your final result. Therefore, it is really important that you get in the habit of doing this. It is also quite important that you do it as soon after the lesson as you can as often we can lose the 'feeling' or 'thought' if we leave it for too long. A good tip is if you are unable to write up your journal straight after the lesson then try and write yourself some bullet points for when you are able to find the time.

Here is a sample of a learning journal:

Tuesday 10th September 2010

Cognitive behavioural Therapy

After learning all my new found skills I have managed to use them at work with a positive outcome. I recognise that I used to end peoples conversations for them which is not really active listening and I realise now that it must have been very frustrating for the patient and my friends.

I also used to have 'on/off' listening I was always thinking about what to do for tea that night and missed half of the conversation. This resulted in me not getting the whole

Introduction to Counselling Skills and Theory

story and having to go back again and ask which didn't really demonstrate that I was a good listener.

I now make a conscious effort to listen and the other day I used the skills learned on the course when listening to an elderly patient who was refusing to eat her meals, and take her medication. I sat with her for a while and gave her some space to talk. She told me all about her days as a school teacher and how much she enjoyed her job.

I asked if everything was okay and told her that I was concerned about how little food she was eating. I used the skills of empathy and humility.

She told me that she was having difficulty swallowing but she didn't like to mention it because everyone seemed to be so busy.

This enabled me to get less solid food for her and to get her medication in liquid form and to communicate this to the doctor who has since instigated some further tests.

Cognitive behavioural therapy was good today. It all makes sense to me. The theory is that our thoughts trigger our feeling which in turn triggers our behaviour. So basically if we have a negative thought we are then going to feel negative, experience negative physical symptoms and behave in a negative way. However if we can change that thought to a more positive one then we will feel more positive and behave in a positive way.

Introduction to Counselling Skills and Theory

I used this with myself. I always think that I am not good enough, that everyone else is better than me. This often left me feeling depressed and physically drained and I would then find myself snapping at people without any reason. I challenged this thought by checking out the evidence. There was no evidence that I am not good enough so I changed that thought to I am actually good enough and almost immediately I felt better and became more sociable with my friends and colleagues.
Wow I am beginning to like this course.

Wednesday 17th September 2010

Person-centred therapy

My friend came round the other day upset, she had been rowing with her husband "He hates me" she cried. I knew this to be untrue as he absolutely adores her. I allowed her to talk using my active listening skills and reflected back some of her words. Once she had finished talking I asked her to tell me about her recent night out for her birthday, she told me that her husband had booked a lovely restaurant and had pre arranged for flowers to be on the table. "That doesn't sound like a man that hates you" I said. I sat with her in silence allowing her to process this new information and I could see instantly that she was beginning to feel better. CBT to the rescue again!!! And I was able to sit with silence!

Introduction to Counselling Skills and Theory

Today we learned another new theory. I didn't realise there was so many different therapeutic models. We learned about Person centred therapy, the founder was Carl Rogers. He believed that as long as you offered the client the space and time and the three core conditions "Empathy, Unconditional Positive regard and Congruence (genuineness)" then this was enough for the client to find solutions to their own problems. Unlike CBT this is a non directive therapy

I think this type of therapy is good but with some people it could be time consuming.

Someone with depression for example could take months to find solutions to their own problems, that is probably why CBT is the evidence based model for people suffering with depression

We did our counselling skills practice (client, helper and observer). I was the helper today and I struggled. There is so much to remember, active listening, mirroring, paraphrasing, clarifying, summarising, offering the core conditions I seem to get a little confused. I get really nervous before I start and then mess up completely but my observer gave me good feedback so I was shocked. I'm not sure I will ever get the hang of this!!!!!

Skills practice:

Introduction to Counselling Skills and Theory

Skills practice is when we practice the skills that we have been taught in the theory part of the course. This usually involves getting into a group of three. One person will take on the role of client, another person a counsellor/helper and another person the observer. The client and the observer will give the trainee counsellor/helper feedback on the practice session.

Feedback is a very significant part of the process as this helps you to grow as a trainee therapist. It is important that the person giving the feedback gives it in a constructive way to empower the trainee rather than disempowering him or her.

Skills practice or role play can cause some anxiety in students, it can feel quite artificial and almost like acting. It can also feel that one has to be perfect and get everything spot on. You don't!

The important thing to remember about making mistakes is that we all do. No-one not even a therapist that has been qualified for several years can be the perfect counsellor. As long as we recognise our unhelpful interventions, most students will still pass the skills element of the course. This process is called reflective practice and you will be reflecting on your own practice in clinical supervision for many years to come.

When taking on the role of client at the early stages of training it is imperative to remember that the person that

Introduction to Counselling Skills and Theory

you are discussing your problem with is a trainee, so therefore not qualified to take on and help you with traumatic or painful issues. These are more appropriately taken to personal therapy. Take to your skills practice problems in the 'here and now' for example "my daughter was bullied at school today" or "my washing machine has broken down." We are all working together as a team and the last thing we want to do is to overwhelm or de-skill our colleagues.

Assignments:

Further on in your training you may be asked to do assignments. The assignments that may be asked of you are:

- A research assignment – This involves researching a particular counselling agency/service or a particular model of therapy or a particular issue that clients may bring to therapy.

Or your tutor may ask you to explore research that has already been done and to evaluate this. Your tutor may ask you to present your findings to the class.

- Taped assignment - This is an assignment that involves either audio or video taping your skills practice. Then reflecting back on this recording and doing a critical evaluation of your work as a trainee counsellor.

Introduction to Counselling Skills and Theory

I will be giving some guidance on how to do this later on in the book, to further support you training.

Most counselling courses are evaluated by a portfolio of your work. However some have now included an exam at the end. It may be worth asking when you apply to go on the course what the assessment criteria is.

Written or computer test.

If you are asked to take a small test this usually involves multiple choice questions or to read a scenario and answer a question about how you would work with this client, for example: what is deemed ethical in this particular situation.

Don't worry too much about this as it will only cover what you have already learned on your course.

Personal development groups:

These may sometimes be known as process groups and may be part of your course. The class particularly if it is a large class may be divided into two and this is when you may go off with your group and process different parts of your learning or discuss issues that are affecting your learning or issues that you find that you are having problems with.

Introduction to Counselling Skills and Theory

The tutor may facilitate a session to help you to explore self. I have put some tools in this book that give an example of the tools that you may use for self exploration.

Personal Therapy and Placements:

As you progress to your diploma year you will be expected to engage in your own personal therapy. This again can be a daunting experience for a trainee and many of you might say 'but I don't know what to take' or 'I don't have any problems at the moment'.

It is an essential part of your training and if it is a criterion for your course then you will not pass without it so get it booked in as soon as you can. Don't worry if you don't know what to take, explain to your therapist that you are a counsellor in training and need to meet your personal therapy requirements and s/he will help you to explore what might be beneficial for you to work through. Don't forget your therapist will have once been where you are.

Another requirement at diploma level will be to find a placement and a clinical supervisor. This is so that you can begin to use your new found skills with 'real' clients supported by a clinical supervisor.

From my experience as a trainee counsellor, trainer and clinical supervisor this is the scariest part of the training, and one of the questions that I am asked the most is "what if I damage the client?" Well, as long as you are

Introduction to Counselling Skills and Theory

using the skills that you have learnt, as long as you are working safely and ethically then this is unlikely to happen. Clinical supervision will support you in ensuring that you are working safely, ethically and within your limitations. Also very rarely will a client let you take them to where they do not want to go.

As daunting as counselling training might sound it is also very rewarding. The emotional growth that you will experience that helps you to function more healthily personally, witnessing the growth of your colleagues and eventually your clients is well worth the journey.

Enjoy your journey!

Introduction to Counselling Skills and Theory

Chapter 2
What is counselling

Many people ask me what is the difference between counselling and psychotherapy?

There have been many a dispute between professionals that there is a difference, and likewise that there is not, and this debate will probably go on for a while to come. I will explain my understanding, as it stands today.

The roots of psychotherapy once lay in the medical and psychiatric professions, whereas counselling developed as a grassroots movement.

The profession has now reached a level where these two disciplines are practically indistinguishable from each other.

Introduction to Counselling Skills and Theory

It is now accepted by most professional bodies that *"it is not possible to make a generally accepted distinction between the two"*.

There are, traditionally, four elements which were meant to distinguish between psychotherapy and counselling.

- Psychotherapy is for deeper seated problems

- Psychotherapy has a different type of dynamic between therapist and client

- Psychotherapy generally lasts for a longer time than counselling

- Psychotherapy takes place in a 'medical' setting but counselling takes place in an 'educational' setting

However, more counsellors are now working with deep seated issues and doing longer term therapy and there are counsellors in a medical setting and psychotherapists in an educational setting. The difference between the two is becoming harder and harder to define.

The important thing to remember about therapeutic counselling is that:

(1) True counselling takes place when a person enlists the help of a counsellor in order to deal effectively with a problem or problems currently experienced

Introduction to Counselling Skills and Theory

(2) Presenting problems may be related to the past or childhood events

(3) They may be anticipated future events or related problems which cause anxiety or worry.

(4) The client has to acknowledge implicitly that they have reached an impasse through which they require help.

The first thing we need to know when training to become a counsellor or psychotherapist is the difference between counselling and helping.

For many years you may have had friends and family come to you with problems and you may feel that you are already counselling them. However, I would suggest that you have maybe been helping them and perhaps using counselling skills.

There is a clear difference between helping, advising and supporting friends and family and entering into a professional relationship with a client as a therapist.

First of all we will look at the difference between friendship and counselling:

INTERACTIONS WITH FRIENDS:

Introduction to Counselling Skills and Theory

With a friend you choose to share a relationship which is open-ended and mutually interdependent.

You can both be your genuine selves, warts and all. You are subjective and spontaneous. You can both share personal experiences. You alternate between helper and helped, give and take.

You can both be positive or negative. You may disagree with each other and offload problems on to each other. You can both make yourselves vulnerable and feel safe.

You can both feel physically, emotionally and spiritually close. There can be a mutual love which may be platonic or erotic.

INTERACTIONS WITH CLIENTS:

A client makes the choice to see you for a purpose. Roles are not interchangeable. They are a short term contract with an agenda.

The relationship depends on the counsellor establishing rapport and trust. Empathy and a non judgmental attitude are required from the counsellor.

Active listening is used by the counsellor to encourage the client to talk. They reflect back feelings, emotions and facts sensitively, accurately and objectively.

Introduction to Counselling Skills and Theory

The counsellor enables the client to cope with difficulties, to look at options, to move on and to change.
The counsellor will be working towards the end of the relationship in a positive way, but leaving the door open for further discussion should the client want it.

It is also important in counselling training to look at the difference between counselling and helping::

Counselling can be defined as:

a   Providing help and support and an understanding listener for someone who is concerned or perplexed.

b   Creating a climate so that the 'client' feels accepted, non-defensive, and able to talk freely about himself and his feelings (begins to build a trusting relationship).

c   Helping the client to gain clearer insight into himself and his situation so that he is better able to help himself and draw on his resources.

Helping can be defined as:

- Listening sympathetically

- Giving information

Introduction to Counselling Skills and Theory

- Teaching

- Giving advice

- Advocating

Whereas counselling can be seen as a process and a set of activities and methods employed within a specific relationship:

- ✓ It is person-centred

- ✓ It involves an emphasis on self-help and choice

- ✓ It is explorative

- ✓ It is challenging in a supportive way

- ✓ It is non-judgemental

- ✓ It involves confidentiality

- ✓ It is based on an agreement or contract

- ✓ It focuses on problems in living

According to the British Association for Counselling and psychotherapy (BACP)

Introduction to Counselling Skills and Theory

"People become engaged in counselling when a person occupying regularly or temporarily the role of counsellor offers or agrees explicitly to offer time, attention and respect to another person or persons temporarily in the role of client."

However, counselling skills can be used in many different professions or settings. Counselling skills are a necessity when working in public services such as:

Nursing
Social Work
Mentoring/Advising/Advocacy

To name but a few, these settings are often 'helping' settings. They are important roles but not where more formal counselling is used.

Counselling differs from other forms of helping in various ways as follows:

1. In helping, the helper is seen as the expert, whereas in counselling the counsellor sees the client as the person who knows the answer to their own difficulty.

2. Counselling skills can be used in all forms of helping and only when a client enters into a counselling contract does it cease to be the use of counselling skills and becomes counselling.

Introduction to Counselling Skills and Theory

3. Confidentiality is part of the contract for counselling and is required to build up the counselling relationship. This issue is not always necessary for helping to take place.

4. It is an ethical requirement for supervision of the counselling work which is not always necessary for helping.

5. Counselling is distinguished from other forms of helping by the emphasis it places upon:

- Enabling those in difficulty to express their experience of their situations in their own terms.

- Enabling them to have their own perception understood and acknowledged by the counsellor.

- Helping the person being counselled to formulate and work towards his/her own solution to his/her own difficulties.

6. The relationship is crucial to counselling and the counsellor needs to have their 'own house in order' - whereas a helper is not necessarily affected by their own difficulties.

It may be helpful to think of the difference between counselling and helping as:

Introduction to Counselling Skills and Theory

'Helping is usually practical, learning a new skill, gaining new information, practical help with difficulties or social interaction.'

Whereas:

'Counselling is not authoritarian. Counsellor and client 'travel the same road together'. A journey that may result in change'

Counselling is not:

- ✘ Being a friend
- ✘ Caring in a parental way
- ✘ 'Treating' or 'healing' someone like a doctor
- ✘ Instructing or Teaching
- ✘ Advising
- ✘ Giving guidance
- ✘ Just using counselling skills

"COUNSELLING IS NOT HELPING PEOPLE MAKE WISE DECISIONS, BUT HELPING THEM TO MAKE DECISIONS WISELY!"

Introduction to Counselling Skills and Theory

> **THOUGHTS:**
>
> Were you aware of the difference?
>
> What would be the possible consequences of dealing with a client's problems in the same way as you do friends?
>
> How might your personal and professional relationships change if you stopped helping and advising and just listened?

Introduction to Counselling Skills and Theory

Chapter 3
Body Language & Communication

Good listening skills are at the heart of developing effective client/therapist relationships, and of course client/helper relationship. Our body language as a listener is important both when you are speaking and when a client is speaking to you. This is sometimes known as 'physical attending' or 'attending behaviour'.

Body messages or body language are messages you can send with your face and other parts of your body. When we are communicating with another person we will be presenting not only our words but also other non verbal communications such as:

BODY LANGUAGE

EYE CONTACT

EXPRESSION (Eyes, Mouth)

Introduction to Counselling Skills and Theory

ATTITUDE (sitting, standing, slumped)

VOICE (Tone, pitch, Volume)

PERSONAL SPACE

GESTURES

Good body Language is the most important thing that you can offer a client to emphasise that you are listening to what they are saying.

Words are only a very small part of communication. While you are saying the words, your body is speaking volumes. In fact did you know that words are only a small percentage of your communication, the tone of your voice and your body language are what people notice the most when you are talking to them.

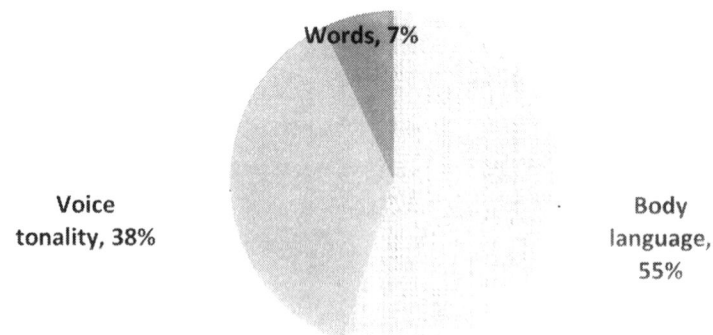

Introduction to Counselling Skills and Theory

To be a rewarding person with whom to talk to you need physically to convey your receptiveness and interest. Voice and body language increases the chances of you being perceived as a rewarding listener. Your body language as a listener is important both when clients and you speak.

Some of the main non verbal ways in which you can demonstrate your interest and your attention as a listener are as follows:

AVAILABILITY- Being totally available to the client and not distracted by other things

RELAXED BODYPOSTURE- (without slumping or slouching)

PHYSICAL OPENNESS- Facing the person, not only with your face but with your body. Uncrossed arms and legs, is known as physical openness.

SLIGHT FORWARD LEAN- Leaning forward is a sign of your involvement. BUT be careful not to invade the client's space.

GOOD EYE CONTACT- Good eye contact means looking in your client's direction so that you allow the possibility of your eyes meeting reasonably often. BUT do not stare.

Introduction to Counselling Skills and Theory

APPROPRIATE FACIAL EXPRESSION- A friendly relaxed facial expression, including a smile, usually demonstrates interest. BUT remember if your client comes in distressed or weeping a smile may not be appropriate.

USE OF HEAD NODS-This lets the client know you are hearing what is being said.

REMEMBER. POSITIVE LISTENING IS NOT JUST HEARING!!!!!

Other messages are:

Verbal messages — These are messages expressed in words — for example what you say when you respond to clients.

Voice messages — These messages relate to how you talk — for example loudly or softly.

Touch messages - Touch is a special kind of body message involving physical contact with another.

Action messages — Action messages are what you do as contrasted with what you say or how you say it: for example, keeping your appointments and starting on time.

Is your body language helping or hindering the message you want to get across? Non-verbal behaviour often

Introduction to Counselling Skills and Theory

mismatches verbal assertions. Check that your body language is congruent with, or/and that it matches, the verbal communication.

Watch out for 'leakage': the cues which give away your feelings despite your attempts to control or disguise them. This needs practice; leakage is confusing rather than 'wrong'

Try disclosing your feelings verbally - paradoxically this can be strengthening. It does not necessarily make you vulnerable.

Other things to consider are:

Posture. Do you hold yourself upright and well-balanced? Or do you slouch, hunch your shoulders, stand on one foot, sit on one buttock? It is impossible to be assertive standing off-balance

Proximity, distance, height. Get to know your own personal space and be sensitive to that of others. Find out whether positioning yourself closer to or further away from the other person is more effective. Ideally, stand or sit directly in front of the other person.

Eyes. Eye contact is the most significant aspect of non-verbal communication to the sighted. Aim for a steady relaxed contact. Avoid an intrusive stare or a shifting gaze

Introduction to Counselling Skills and Theory

Mouth and jaw. Common leakages are the clenched jaw signalling tension or aggression, and the false or fixed smile. Watch for the automatic smile which says 'please don't be angry', or 'I don't want to appear nasty' when you have some straight talking to do

Voice. Notice how changes in pitch and tone can signal timidness, whining, sarcasm, etc. Breathing and relaxation will help you to project your voice assertively

Gestures. Some gestures bring what you are saying to life - others are irritating or distracting. Fiddling conveys nervousness, tapping or chopping indicates impatience or anger

Think about how you feel inside.

If you are having a bad day or have just received some upsetting news or are angry at someone then this can present itself in your body language or tone of voice when you meet with your client. Be especially mindful of this.

Your body language makes an impression on others and it has an important impact on you.

Communication skills
Receiving messages – active listening.

Active listening involves giving the person our full attention and conveying that we are doing so.

Introduction to Counselling Skills and Theory

The Skills for active listening include:

- Clearing away 'baggage', thoughts and feelings brought in from previous happenings and experiences.

- Attending to the content in the words, and the feeling behind them, for the words are not the whole message.

- Checking out that you are picking up the message accurately. Asking for clarification, summarising and checking out inconsistencies.

- Listening for themes and essential facts. It is sometimes easy to be distracted by side issues.

- Listening positively. Avoiding prejudices or blocks to hearing what the person is really saying. Listening with balance and not simply for points to challenge or disagree with.

However, the RECEIVER can reduce the effectiveness of communication by:

- Jumping to conclusions and reacting prematurely. Being judgemental.

- Changing the subject, deflecting the point the sender is trying to make.

Introduction to Counselling Skills and Theory

- Interrupting or talking too much them self.

- Latching on to minor details while ignoring the main points.

- Switching off or ignoring what is said.

- Failing to check out assumptions or ask for clarification; not summarising what she has heard.

- Not recognising, or responding to, the level of the sender's message, eg being flippant

- Being defensive rather than open.

> **Thoughts:**
>
> How often do you look at the other person's non verbal cues, their body language, their facial expression, their tone of voice when listening to them?

Introduction to Counselling Skills and Theory

Chapter 4
Listening Skills

As discussed in the previous chapter good listening skills are at the heart of developing effective client/therapist relationships. It is surprising to most of us when we learn that although we always thought we were good listeners, we actually were not using the 'eyes' and 'ears' that we were born with as effectively as we could.

There are some blocks to good listening that you need to be mindful of when working with clients.

You may have difficulty hearing the words of another when:

- The person's views are different from yours.

- The person's culture, education or work experience deviate from yours.

Introduction to Counselling Skills and Theory

- It is not easy to follow the thoughts expressed because you do not know the vocabulary.

- The person speaks with a dialect or accent.

- The accent or appearance of the speaker is extreme in some way.

- You have heard the discourse before, by the speaker or someone else.

- The thoughts or feelings being expressed shock you or cause you to feel anxious.

- You realise you are out of your depth in trying to converse with another.

- The person is telling you something you do not want to hear.

- The environment is noisy, or frequent interruptions occur.

- You are experiencing stress or discomfort to any degree (physical, emotional, social).

- The words of the speaker belie his or her actions or true feelings.

Introduction to Counselling Skills and Theory

- Your emotions influence your rational approach to the discourse.

- You will have to admit an error.

- You realise an apology from you should be forthcoming.

- The values you support are under attack.

- You are self-centred and hear only your own voice.

- The news or outcome of a situation is not good.

- The needs of another will demand a commitment or involvement by you.

- The sense of hearing is impaired or lost permanently.

- You decide you dislike the person, with insufficient information or evidence.

One of the things that you will be encouraged to develop during your training is your 'Active listening' skills.

Active listening is "What we pay attention to in the person we are helping."

This is one of the key ingredients in any helping relationship. It is impossible to be helpful if you are not

Introduction to Counselling Skills and Theory

actively listening. It is about watching and listening to all the signals the client is giving, both verbally and visually.

It is some of the things that enable us to "step into their world", "hear what they're not saying" and "understand their thoughts, behaviour and feelings."

It is listening to the following:

- Voice quality - soft, hard, confident, timid, strong, weak etc.

- Breathing - deep, shallow, sobbing, snatched, relaxed etc.

- Facial expression - Relaxed, tense, afraid, happy, disgust etc.

- Whether they are talking or silent?

- The story they are telling and how they are telling it?

ALL OF THIS FORMS A PICTURE OF THE CLIENTS WORLD AND THE CLIENTS THOUGHTS, FEELINGS AND BEHAVIOUR.

Active listening is not passive. It is a positive encouragement to a person to talk by means of friendly body language, nods, eye contact and non-para verbals (umming and arring)

Introduction to Counselling Skills and Theory

Active listening is not every day listening when we are prepared to listen to another in exchange for others listening in return, in a trade off. It is being prepared to receive whatever the speaker wishes to reveal, avoiding switching off signs such as facial expressions of disbelief or shock, fidgeting and distraction actions. It does not mean sitting in judgement or blaming the person.

Active listening involves giving the person our full attention and conveying that we are doing so.

Good communication skills take practice and you will have lots of practice on this course, inside and outside of the classroom.

Oh didn't I tell you this? You will be encouraged to use your skills at home too, but be prepared for your family to say "Don't come home and counsel me". You are not of course counselling them just practising your newly developed communication & counselling skills on them!

There are many barriers to good listening and barriers to good listening can be external or internal:

External - Consider the environment you are working in. Consider the noise levels.

Internal - The Mental Process. For example:

- Worries and anxieties lead to lack of concentration

Introduction to Counselling Skills and Theory

- Thoughts can be triggered by the client and you can go down your own road.

- Helper/counsellor can be tired

- Client can force the listener to stereotype

- You may not like the way the person talks or the content of the story and turn off.

- Feelings can be triggered in the helper/counsellor that are uncomfortable. (These need to be attended to in the helper/counsellors own time)

- There are times that a listener does not hear because he is not prepared to hear. If he listens to his own feelings it may be due, for example to his own anxiety

To listen with undivided attention it requires a level of maturity and self acceptance. It needs you to be mindful of the following:

- Pay attention to the smallest detail.

- Be aware of the clients thinking feeling and behaviour.

Introduction to Counselling Skills and Theory

- Do not be anxious as you will hear less

- Don't cut into the conversation too often. Respect silences

Some of the other barriers that you may want to consider are as follows:

"ON/OFF" LISTENING – Listening to some of the story and then switching off into your own private world.

"RED FLAG" LISTENING – This is when we are listening until we hear words that upset us. For example: 'police', 'union'. 'should or musts' 'unfaithful etc. They are words that provoke a negative response within ourselves. When this happens we stop listening.

"OPEN EARS CLOSED MIND" LISTENING – Sometimes we decide rather quickly that either the subject or the speaker is boring, or think we know what s/he will say so we automatically switch off, as we will hear nothing new.

"GLASSY EYED" LISTENING – We look at the person and appear to be listening but our mind is elsewhere. We drop back into the comfort of our own thoughts. We have a dreamy expression which is an instant give away that the person is not listening.

Introduction to Counselling Skills and Theory

"TOO-DEEP-FOR-ME" LISTENING – This is when we are listening to ideas that are too complex and complicated, we can shut off and stop listening, rather than ask the speaker to explain what s/he means.

"MATTER OVER MIND" LISTENING – We do not like to have our opinions and judgements challenged, therefore when a speaker says something that clashes with what we think, we may unconsciously stop listening,

"SUBJECT CENTRED" LISTENING – Sometimes we may concentrate on the problem and not the person, detail and fact about the problem, rather than what s/he is saying about him/herself.

"PENCIL" LISTENING – Trying to put down on paper everything the speaker is saying. The speaker is faster so we lose a percentage of what they are saying.

"HUBNUB" LISTENING – Sometimes there are many distraction when we listen for example noise, movement of people or other matters taking up our attention.

REMEMBER: Being aware of the above barriers and reminding ourselves about them frequently are the first steps to becoming a good listener.

YOU ARE NOT LISTENING TO ME WHEN ....

- You do not care about me.

Introduction to Counselling Skills and Theory

- You say you understand before you know me well enough.

- You have an answer to my problem before I've finished telling you what my problem is.

- You cut me off before I have finished speaking.

- You find me boring and do not tell me.

- You feel critical of my vocabulary, grammar or accent.

- You are dying to tell me something

- You tell me about your experience making mine seem unimportant

- You are communicating to someone else in the room

- You refuse my thanks by saying that you haven't really done anything.

YOU ARE LISTENING TO ME WHEN..........

- You come quietly into my private world and let me be me.

- You really try to understand me even if I'm not making much sense.

Introduction to Counselling Skills and Theory

- You grasp my point of view even when it goes against your own sincere convictions.

- You realise that the hour I took from you as left you a bit tired and drained.

- You allow me the dignity of making my own decisions even though you think that they might be wrong.

- You do not take my problem from me, but allow me to deal with it in my own way.

- You hold back your desire to give me 'good advice'.

- You do not offer me religious solace when you sense I am not ready for it.

- You give me enough room to discover for myself what is going on.

- You accept my gift of gratitude by telling me how good it makes you feel to know you have been helpful.

Thoughts:

What are your barriers to listening?

How might you overcome them?

Introduction to Counselling Skills and Theory

LISTEN

When I ask you to listen to me and you start giving advice you have not done what I asked. When I ask you to listen to me and you begin to tell me why I should not feel that way, you have failed me, strange as that may seem.

Listen! All I asked was that you listen. Not talk or do - just hear me. Advice is cheap; 10 cents will get you both Dear Abby and Billy Graham in the same newspaper and that I can do for myself. I am not helpless, maybe discouraged and-faltering but not helpless.

When you do something for me that I can and need to do for myself, you contribute to my fear and weakness. But when you accept as a simple fact that I do feel what I feel no matter how irrational, then I quit trying to convince you and can get about the business of understanding what's behind this irrational feeling and when that is clear, the answers are obvious and I do not need advice

Irrational feelings make sense when we understand what is behind them. Perhaps that is why prayer works, sometimes, for some people because God is mute and he does not give advice or try to fix things. "They" listen and let you work it out for yourself. So, please listen and just hear me. And, if you want to talk, wait a minute for your turn and I will listen to you.

ANONYMOUS

Introduction to Counselling Skills and Theory

Chapter 5
Personal development tools

Often students will ask the question "Why do we need to do personal development in counselling training?" Let me ask you the question who are you and who can you be for others as you are now?

By that I mean:

- What judgements do you have?

- What difficulties do you experience?

- What are your weaknesses?

- How can you develop your strengths?

- Do you like yourself?

Introduction to Counselling Skills and Theory

- What blocks your learning and your ability to help others?

- Have you reached your full potential?

- What is your full potential?

- What do you do when you feel angry?

- Is it okay to be angry?

- Are you aware of your prejudices?

- How do you usually get your needs met?

- What has happened to you in your life and how does it impact on your relationships with others?

- How well do you feel emotionally and mentally?

- How do you take care of yourself?

Personal development is an ongoing process of self improvement. It is about becoming aware of the 'what and why' about ourselves. In a sense it is about 'getting to know you' on a deeper level, such as:

- What do we feel about ourselves?

- What are our fears?

Introduction to Counselling Skills and Theory

- What is our sexuality?

- What are our values and beliefs?

- What are our morals and ethics?

- What is our cultural background?

- What are our attitudes to race, religion, and social class?

- What do we struggle with or find challenging in people?

There are many questions that we need to ask ourselves when training to be a counsellor. We need to understand ourselves to enable us to understand others and to understand what areas or issues we would struggle with.

It is important to have self-awareness when training as a counsellor and when practicing as a counsellor for the following reasons:

- To enable a counsellor to reflect on their practice

- To enable a counsellor to remain emotionally detached from the relationship s/he is developing with a client

Introduction to Counselling Skills and Theory

- To assess personal strengths, feelings, thoughts and limitations as they relate to other people

- To be aware of a sense of personal familiarity

- To gain a knowledge of our own beliefs, attitudes and values and how they may impact on others

- To gain a better understanding of self

If we did not do this can you imagine the complications that may arise when practicing as a therapist:

- What would happen in the therapy room if someone came into the room with differing beliefs to you?

- How would you cope with a client with a similar issue to you?

- What would you do if a client swore?

- What would you do if you found a client attractive?

Introduction to Counselling Skills and Theory

- What if a client came in with a personality trait that irritated you?

- How might you deal with a client that was angry at you and you struggled with people who were angry?

Personal development tools are helpful when exploring 'self', which is a necessity in counselling training. As uncomfortable as this may feel at the time in the long term you will see the benefits. Also the benefit of doing this and using the tools given to you by your tutor is that you are developing a therapeutic toolbox for when you begin your client work.

The tools that you use for your own personal development can often help clients to explore too. They can help you to get to know your client better, enable you to step into their world and subsequently support them in their goal of treatment. Be mindful though when using tools with your client that it is to benefit them and not because you are stuck.

The following tool is to help you to look at your own health at the moment both psychologically and mentally. When in practice it is extremely important to monitor your own mental health to enable you to practice safely. If any issues arise then you are able to work through them to ensure that they do not impact on your client work.

Introduction to Counselling Skills and Theory

MY MENTAL HEALTH CV

My current problems:	My life – significant events:
My strengths:	

What helps:	What doesn't help:

My future direction

Introduction to Counselling Skills and Theory

So let's look at the mental health CV. Firstly you will be exploring:

- Any current problems that you have in your own life.

    "My daughter is playing up at the moment"

- Then you may like to look at the strengths that you have to manage these difficulties.

    "My family are very supportive"

    "I am good at putting boundaries in"

- What helps?

    ✓ *Relaxation*

    ✓ *Being with others*

    ✓ *Reading*

    ✓ *Getting out*

    ✓ *Talking*

    ✓ *Imagery (for thoughts)*

- What doesn't help?

Introduction to Counselling Skills and Theory

- ✘ *Alcohol*
- ✘ *Over eating*
- ✘ *Staying in bed*
- ✘ *Withdrawing*

- What life significant events have created this difficulty?

    "Trying to look after my sick mother"

    "Husband doing more overtime"

    "Equals less time with children"

    - And last but not least what is your future direction?

        - ✓ *Education*
        - ✓ *Personal Development*
        - ✓ *Work*
        - ✓ *Therapy*
        - ✓ *Spending more time with the children*

Introduction to Counselling Skills and Theory

- ✓ *Tightening the boundaries with the children*

- ✓ *Gaining more support from family*

That is the beginning of you looking at you and what is going on in your life currently. What level of support you have and where you may want to get extra support.

It also helps you to see what tools you have to support you, what tools or strategies that are not helpful and to explore significant events that may have contributed to your problems.

Last but not least what your future goals are.

This is the beginning of your personal development. Well done!

Introduction to Counselling Skills and Theory

Chapter 6
Core Conditions

Theory and exploring therapeutic models is important when training to be a counsellor. Helping is a skilled and responsible role. Anyone wanting to improve their helping skills needs to look at three aspects which contribute to their performance as a helper:

- Theory

- Skills

- The personality of the helper (personal development)

Theories are about how and why humans behave as they do. If we did not have an understanding of ourselves and others would we truly be able to offer a safe and conducive relationship with others?

Introduction to Counselling Skills and Theory

Last but not least theories help us to provide evidence for why we do what we do, what models work best with what issue, and how we can evaluate our results.

You will learn about several different therapeutic models during your training, however unless you are doing an integrative or eclectic course (which means learning lots of different models), you will probably follow one model during your course. More will be explained later in this book.

I am introducing the core conditions now because I believe that they are an important part of the therapeutic relationship and they are the foundations of any counsellor's work. It does not matter what model that you eventually come to practice I consider that the core conditions are the basics for your practice. These need to always be in place.

Carl Rogers the founder of 'Person Centred Therapy' talks about there being three core conditions needed to be a counsellor. These core conditions are what help us to develop a safe and trusting relationship with our clients.

They are:

EMPATHY

CONGRUENCE

Introduction to Counselling Skills and Theory

AND

UNCONDITIONAL POSITIVE REGARD

The definition of these core conditions are as follows:

EMPATHY - This is trying to see the world of another person from their point of view, otherwise known as 'stepping into the client's world and feeling what they are feeling'.

CONGRUENCE - This involves the helper being open to his or her own feelings as much as possible. It means being 'my real self' without front or facade, without acting like an expert.

UNCONDITIONAL POSITIVE REGARD - This core condition is also called non-judgemental, warmth or acceptance. It means that we must be able to totally accept the person we are trying to help as a worthwhile human being.

That is the simplified definition; however within your training you will explore these core conditions more profoundly. This is to enable you to practice these skills both in the classroom and in your personal life.

That does not mean however that you go home and counsel everyone. These are counselling skills that you may be able to use in your work and home environment

Introduction to Counselling Skills and Theory

to improve both your listening skills, communication skills and of course interpersonal relationship skills.

What Empathy is:

"Empathy is the ability to put yourself in another person's shoes. It is the process of knowing someone deeply, echoing their feelings and experiences without being judgmental or evaluative."

"The Indians expressed it as walking a mile in another person's moccasins"

"Empathy is one of Carl Rogers core conditions described as a necessity in the therapeutic relationship. He believes that by demonstrating these core conditions, the client will have the ability to reach their own solution to their problem."

It is defined as:-

- The power of understanding and imaginatively entering into another person's feelings. – **Collins English Dictionary.**

- Behaviours in which convey that you understand the other person's world as they are experiencing it. – **Hopson & Scally (1980)**

Introduction to Counselling Skills and Theory

- We begin to perceive the events and experiences of life 'as if' they were parts of our own life. – **Truax and Carkhuff (1967)**

Empathy is a way of being with others and a communication skill.

Basic empathy is listening carefully to the client and then communicating understanding of what the client is feeling and the behaviour underlying these feelings. It's the helper's way of saying I am with you.

"You feel ………………… because……….."

Of course, the exact words of the formula are not important. They merely provide a framework for communicating understanding.

Hints for improving empathy:-

- Give yourself time to think.

- Give yourself time to reflect on what has been said.

- Ask yourself what feelings is this person expressing?' What is the core message?

- Use short responses. The beginner may become long winded.

Introduction to Counselling Skills and Theory

- Gear your response to the client. Helpers are more empathic when their language is in tune with the language of the client.

Suggestions for the Use of Basic Empathy are:-

- ✓ Remember that empathy is, ideally, a "way of being" and not just a professional role or communication skill.

- ✓ Attend carefully, both physically and psychologically, and listen to the client's point of view.

- ✓ Try to set aside your biases and judgments for the moment and walk, as it were, in the shoes of your client.

- ✓ As the client speaks, listen for the core messages.

- ✓ Listen to both verbal and non verbal messages and their contexts.

- ✓ Respond fairly frequently, but briefly, to the client's core messages.

- ✓ Be flexible and tentative enough so that the client does not feel pinned down.

Introduction to Counselling Skills and Theory

- ✓ Be gentle, but keep the client focused on important issues.

- ✓ Respond to the main features of core messages - experiences, behaviours, and feelings - unless there is reason for emphasizing one over the others.

- ✓ Gradually move towards the exploration of sensitive topics and feelings.

- ✓ After responding with empathy attend carefully to cues that either confirm or deny the accuracy of your response.

Some of the skills needed to demonstrate Empathy:

- **Good open body language and eye contact** — and an ability to 'listen to' others body language, facial expression and tonality as well as 'the words'

- **Good listening skills and awareness of own barriers to listening** — Empathy is being able to listen so intently and being able to identify so closely that you experience the other person's situation, thoughts and emotions.

> "If we were supposed to talk more than we listen, we would have two mouths and one ear" — Mark Twain.

Introduction to Counselling Skills and Theory

- **An ability to step into a client's internal frame of reference** — and communicate this experience to the client.

- **Good reflection, clarifying and paraphrasing skills** and an ability to reflect back the 'feeling' content rather than behaviour or circumstance.

- **Good self awareness** — to enable you to tune into the thoughts or feelings of another and tune out one's own judgments. Being aware of what your feelings are, which may be different to the client's and being able to separate those.

> "Roger's believes that to accurately perceive and feel the clients feelings and personal meanings, then convey this to them, will assist the client in achieving greater understanding and control over their behaviour and circumstance."

What Empathy is not:

- ✘ Changing the topic responses
- ✘ "I know better than you" responses
- ✘ Judgmental responses
- ✘ Advising

Introduction to Counselling Skills and Theory

- ✘ Discounting or premature responses

- ✘ Psychoanalysis or diagnosis

- ✘ Questioning or telling your own story

- ✘ Sympathy

> Sympathy is what one person gives another - because THEY want all the details!
>
> Sympathy is to pity - Empathy is to appreciate fully!
>
> Sympathy can be condescending and not always gratefully accepted - Empathy is showing the person that you fully understand and feel!

Empathy is conveyed by:

- ✓ Appropriate body language

- ✓ Active Listening

- ✓ Reflecting

- ✓ Paraphrasing

Introduction to Counselling Skills and Theory

- ✓ Summarising

- ✓ Clarifying

- ✓ Open Questions

- ✓ Behavioural Mirroring – Smiling when the other person smiles, frowning when the other person frowns.

Personal qualities needed:

Understanding & Warmth

SUMMARY:

Empathic Understanding involves looking at the world from the client's point of view.

Empathy is not the same as sympathy/cheering up/saying 'you'll be alright'. It is more to do with being sensitive to other people's needs and being concerned about what they want.

Empathy can enable other people's messages to get through to us clearly, and our messages to get through to them, even though the client and the counsellor may have very different backgrounds, experiences, expectations and values

Introduction to Counselling Skills and Theory

What congruence is:

Congruence is being your 'real self' with clients. It is about being sincere. Sincerity means that we behave honestly with people, so that they know where they stand with us and can trust us not to try to manipulate them.

This requires us to be honest about the things people don't want to hear, as well as the things they do; but clients need to be able to trust that comments will be made with empathy and without implying loss of acceptance.

We need to maintain our own integrity, so that others feel that they are dealing with a genuine person; in doing this, we not only model self-respect, but also show respect for them, by not pretending to be something we are not.

The Congruent State is the concept of authentic genuiness. When a person is complete they can live, work and experience life from a position of doing whatever they feel is right for them without the judgements of their past interfering with the present.

Introduction to Counselling Skills and Theory

It's the point when you express yourself in such a way that it is clean and comes straight from the heart. At times there is confusion, and lack of clarity, but that is part of the struggle. That is finding out who you are.

It may be about sharing your feelings with your client, letting them know that you are stepping into their world.

Example

You are with a client, and you feel weepy. Go with that, and express it to the client. Say "that sounds quite sad, that sounds a difficult place to be in." You can on the other hand be silent, and let the tears flow.

It's that experiencing of two people together

We cannot always offer congruence when we are over analysing our clients, sometimes it is just sitting with their pain. To over analyse means that we may lose our ability to feel at gut level.

This is where silence is important because if we try to put the gut stuff into words, by the time it comes out it may totally change. This may because our judgements may come seeping through.

The challenge is to be congruent. It's about being free and as open as we can with ourselves.

Introduction to Counselling Skills and Theory

However there are some feelings that may not have any therapeutic value to share.

If you are angry with your client, or feel angry within yourself it would not be honest to stamp your feet and say " you have to work harder. I'm pissed off with you at the moment" That would be your stuff seeping into the therapy room.

It is important to remember that the client is doing the best s/he can.

Our job is to communicate to that client that there seems to be some frustration around what they are saying, something that is blocking the process, and then spending some time exploring what this might be about.

This time belongs to the client. Our anger belongs somewhere else, therapy, supervision, the gym or wherever or whatever you do to manage your own anger.

The aim is to communicate, as honestly as possible thus building a therapeutic alliance.

Always explore feelings with your client to avoid them is being incongruent. Try to leave the head behind.

Don't try to be the 'perfect counsellor' or people please this is being incongruent.

Introduction to Counselling Skills and Theory

You can only do the best you can do at any particular moment in time. That's living the moment, and being congruent.

Congruence is not as easier as it sounds. Rogers describes it as being the feelings that flow from within to without.

The within is what you are experiencing. e.g. my heart is pounding really quickly. I feel anxious, excited, and uncertain. I feel all these different things. The within is what you feel in your stomach, your gut feeling or your intuition. To listen to your gut feeling whilst listening to the client will enable you to offer congruence and make the right responses.

By being authentic, genuine, by the use of empathic responses, and treating them with respect. You are showing unconditional positive regard.

As a counsellor you are always modelling this ideal state of being congruent

If you are not genuine, congruent, empathic, if you show that all your interventions is based on judgement, that will totally block the relationship and the client will leave.

Every person is a human being first, and they come to us as clients. We are also human. You work within this frame work

Introduction to Counselling Skills and Theory

This is how I see this person, as this other human being, who had to adapt to life, because of his or her conditions of worth. Conditions of worth are conditions which have been placed on them during early child development.

So that's how you see them, working within this framework and Rogers would add 'with no other fixed tools other than being congruent, unconditional, and empathic'.

All the other things that you use are what you make it. E.g. Use the skills that you have being given like the theory, art, music, shapes etc.

Congruence is conveyed by:

- Genuineness
- Immediacy
- Self disclosure
- Appropriate referral
- Challenge
- Confrontation
- Responding naturally

Introduction to Counselling Skills and Theory

- Sharing feelings appropriately

- Being spontaneous

- Not being defensive

- Not pretending to be someone or something you are not

Personal qualities needed:

- Self Awareness

- Good self esteem

- Honesty

- Genuineness

- Knowledge

Unconditional positive regard is:

An accepting attitude of mind which enables us to avoid prejudging people and situations, so that we do not make assumptions about them, but see everyone as an individual, with individual needs.

Acceptance means valuing another person as someone who deserves our attention and respect in their own right

Introduction to Counselling Skills and Theory

- perhaps even more than they, themselves, feel they deserve.

Unconditional positive regard is conveyed by:

- Understanding diversity
- Being Non judgemental
- Acceptance
- Understanding Human behaviour
- Respect
- Self development
- Active listening
- Giving your time
- Remembering the person's name
- Introducing yourself
- Basic courtesies – offering a chair
- Asking questions
- Checking out assumptions

Introduction to Counselling Skills and Theory

- Not interrupting or talking over the person

- Giving positive attention

Personal qualities needed:

- Respect

- Value

- Common Sense

Person centred therapy consists of the client talking about whatever they wish (there is no focus to the therapy or no setting of goals), and it is the job of the therapist to actively listen, offer the core conditions and to paraphrase and clarify what the client has said.

Rogers believed that by offering this environment, the client has a 'safe space' in which to explore their own feelings, and in this act of trying to explain things to another person this would be enough to 'unmuddle' yourself.

However it is not as simple as it seems, it is an art to offer this kind of therapy that requires many years of practice and a great deal of personal development.

However, I believe them to be an essential part of the relationship between yourself and the client. You can

Introduction to Counselling Skills and Theory

have as many tools in your tool box as you like, you can have the skills and training to delve deep into a client's past but without the core conditions in place the client may be unable to develop a warm and trusting relationship with you. The core conditions are a must in any helping relationship.

Never-the less, there is more to offering the core conditions than meets the eye!

Thoughts:

Can you see any difficulties in perhaps being able to offer the three core conditions to a client?

You have a convicted paedophile for a client. How might this leave you feeling?

Do you offer congruence and tell the client that you are horrified by his behaviour?

OR

Do you try and offer unconditional positive regard and risk being dishonest and ungenuine?

Introduction to Counselling Skills and Theory

Rogers would have erred on the side of being genuine as without this element, he would suggest that therapy would be unsuccessful anyway.

My philosophy is that the core conditions are needed to build the relationship with the client, to develop trust and an important part of the information gathering. In my counselling practice they are the foundations to my work.

Introduction to Counselling Skills and Theory

Chapter 7
Reflection, Clarifying, Paraphrasing and Summarising

Part of active listening and communicating empathy to your client is to be able to use the following skills:

- Reflection
- Paraphrasing
- Clarifying
- Summarising

Reflection is to summarise in a few words what the client is saying, usually from a 'feeling' content'.

Example:

"She just bangs around the house and slams the door"

Introduction to Counselling Skills and Theory

"It sounds like you are feeling angry at your wife's behaviour"

It is important then in order to use reflection effectively that you have a good 'feelings' vocabulary.

The purpose is to demonstrate your understanding of how the client might be feeling (or not)

Paraphrasing is quite simply to repeat the content of the other person's words back to them.

It is important to paraphrase without sounding like a parrot and this takes practice.

The purpose of this is to let the client know that you are listening to them and trying to understand. You are in a sense asking if you have got it right.

Clarifying is to seek clarification of your own understanding of the client's world.

Example:

"I have just been made redundant and my wife is threatening to leave me, so I will become single and homeless at the same time. I don't know what to do or how to make things better."

Introduction to Counselling Skills and Theory

"You will become homeless because you will be unable to pay your rent and single if your wife leaves you and you are trying to work out a way of preventing these things from happening?"

The purpose is to demonstrate that you are trying to step into their world.

By rephrasing this it helps the client to understand themselves better by hearing their problem in a different way.

It can help you to clarify things if you are muddled and lack understanding of what the client is saying.

Summarising is quite simply, summarising the main content of the session in short.

- Letting the client know that you have listened
- If the interview needed moving forward
- To ensure that you have understood the problem
- To gather important points together
- To help the client decide which of the points that he wanted to talk about in more detail.

Introduction to Counselling Skills and Theory

▸ To help the client if he was stuck, going around in circles or if he was confused

Silence

One of the difficult skills for counsellors in training as well as indeed many of us is to maintain silence in a listening relationship. We have an automatic urge to jump in and say something, sometimes anything rather than to sit in silence. Culturally we have been taught to be uncomfortable with silence; this can influence the counsellor's use of silence and the client's reactions to it.

However being able to sit in silence with your client is a very important skill.

Silence within counselling has been defined as:

"The temporary absence of any overt verbal or paraverbal communication between counsellor and client within sessions"

To be able to sit in silence with your client is a skill that needs to be taught and learned in any model of training, however **(Mearnes 1997)** stated the following:

"The person-centred counsellor needs to be prepared to listen to silences as well as words, recognising that the silence may help the client focus."

Introduction to Counselling Skills and Theory

Silence can actually be productive and it also places the responsibility of the session in the hands of the client, ensuring that when the silence is broken the session is still focused on the client's agenda.

By breaking the silence due to personal discomfort, the agenda has become the counsellors. Silences occur for a number of reasons.

For the counsellor it can be:

- A deliberate use of silence to encourage the client's self-exploration

- A deliberate use of silence to encourage the client to "carry the burden" of the conversation.

- A use of silence enabling the counsellor to collect her/his own thoughts.

- A natural ending to a phase of discussion.

For the client it can be:

- A time to make connections, to wait for words or images to occur.

- A space in which feelings can be nurtured and allowed to develop.

Introduction to Counselling Skills and Theory

- A space in which the client is able to recover from "here and now" emotions.

- An attempt to elicit a response from the counsellor, such as satisfying a need for approval or advice.

- A use of silence enabling the client to collect her/his own thoughts, remember events, assess values and reflect on feelings.

Silence gives you:

The ability to listen effectively. If you can't resist thinking about what you want to say when listening, focus instead specifically on being silent. You'll be surprised how much your ability to concentrate will improve.

Silence gives you:

A clear view into the hearts of others. Silence gets you out of the way and creates a. space others will fill in with *themselves*. A person's personality becomes apparent in mere hours to days. Assessing a person's character, on the other hand, takes months to years.

Silence gives you:

Wisdom. - One of the BACP qualities needed to practice. While you are listening you are learning not only about

Introduction to Counselling Skills and Theory

the client but also about yourself and your own responses to what the client is saying.

> **Thoughts:**
>
> How might using the skills learned in this chapter help the client?
>
> Sit for a while and think about:
>
> "What type of feeling can cause you to fill the space when there is silence in a conversation?"

Introduction to Counselling Skills and Theory

Chapter 8
Assessments, contracting & boundaries

In the counselling domain there are often arguments for and against using assessment forms in the counselling relationship.

A question often asked of me is "why is it sometimes deemed important to do an assessment before the therapy begins?"

Well there are several reasons for this and they are as follows:

To gain an insight into clients:

- o Life (present and past)

- o Their current problem

- o Their ways of communicating

Introduction to Counselling Skills and Theory

- Their ways of behaving

- Their understanding of their own problems

- Their past and present mental health issues

- History of traumas

- Their drug and alcohol use

- And last but by no means least any issues around risk.

Counselling is like baking a cake without the ingredients we are unable to help the client to bake their cake.

For those of us that work using a more directive therapy, the ingredients also help us to develop a treatment plan and make a decision on what tools and techniques we have that might help this client.

We need information to assess the following:

- If we are able to help this client. Is the issue that they are presenting with, within our limit of expertise?

- If the client has any risk issues that we need to be aware of whilst working with him or her.

Introduction to Counselling Skills and Theory

- What medication the client is on to differentiate between the normal and the side effects of any medications.

- Are there any other professionals involved in their care? To enable us to liaise with them if necessary and with the clients consent and to ensure that the client is not being overloaded with professional help.

- What the clients understanding of counselling is to explore any thoughts of being 'fixed'.

- What is the clients understanding of the problem to assess if the client has their own formulation of their difficulties, and to gain a clear perception into the clients insight of their problems or difficulties.

- What are the client's goals of therapy to explore if these are achievable?

- Childhood and relationship issues to explore any themes/patterns in the client's life.

When working as a counsellor you may devise your own assessment form or use one provided by the organisation that you may be working for.

Here is an example of what may be put on an assessment form:

Introduction to Counselling Skills and Theory

Name:

Address:

Date of birth:

GP:

Marital status & children:

Any other professionals involved in care:

Any child protection issues:

Alcohol or substance misuse:

Prescribed medication:

Mental Health history:

History of self harm or suicide attempts:

Presenting issue:

Clients' formulation of problem/difficulties:

Clients' goal of treatment:

At Diploma level when you are more experienced and have begun to work with people's history or traumas then

Introduction to Counselling Skills and Theory

you may wish to include the following on your assessment:

Family history:

Childhood experiences:

Relationship history:

Any traumas or difficult experiences in your life:

Some organisations may require extra information or you may want to add some extra questions to meet your own personal style of working.

One of the things that I ask clients is "what are your interests and hobbies" which enables me to use this in the therapy sessions i.e using their hobbies and interests metaphorically to enable the client to develop a better insight.

Contracts:

If you are using counselling skills then it is not always necessary to contract with the person that you are helping. However even as a helper, doctor, nurse or friend you may feel that some agreement is needed. Within a counselling relationship it is important to contract with a client. It is essential to be transparent with

Introduction to Counselling Skills and Theory

your client prior to his or her commitment to therapy about what your 'ground rules' are.

In your first session or pre-session you may want to:

- Ask the person you are helping what they expect from you

- Explain what you expect from them (fees, for them to maintain their medication, to not attend your sessions under the influence of drink or illicit drugs, to arrive on time, and what your boundaries are re cancellations or DNA's)

- Explain as clearly as you can your role, the helping that you are qualified to, willing and able to offer.

- Explain your limits i.e. confidentiality, supervision arrangements, whether you are still in training etc.

- Make clear arrangements about:

    ▸ Where the meetings will take place

    ▸ When the meetings will take place

    ▸ How many meetings/sessions there will be

    ▸ How long they will be for i.e 30 minutes/hour

Introduction to Counselling Skills and Theory

> ▸ If there is to be a case review and when

Summarise the points at the end of the first meeting and offer to put in writing and bring to the next meeting if the person wishes.

Other boundaries to explore are:

- Is it acceptable for a client to act out his anger in his session with you?

- Is it acceptable for him to flirt with you?

- Is it acceptable to shout at you?

- Is it acceptable for him/her to touch you?

- Is it acceptable for him/her to ask about your personal life?

Contracting is something you can use in your everyday life. Have you ever had a friend visit or telephone you with a problem and you have gone around in circles and felt exhausted when s/he has left?

You can even contract with friends when they come to you with a problem, although they are not aware that you are doing it.

Introduction to Counselling Skills and Theory

I may say to my friends, "come on in I will put the kettle on, I have got about an hour is that okay?"

This way I prevent myself from 'burn out' and usually what cannot be resolved in an hour cannot be resolved that day, you can just end up going around in circles.

> **Thoughts:**
>
> Do contracts improve helping when counselling skills are used or not?
>
> What are your experiences of contracts in other helping relationships?
>
> Is there anything other than what is discussed in this chapter that you might add to your assessment or any boundaries you may want to include in your contracting?

Introduction to Counselling Skills and Theory

Chapter 9
Open and Closed Questions

The arguments for and against questioning in counselling, are similar to the arguments for and against assessment.

Wrongly used, questions can lead to passive clients who implicitly or explicitly expect their counsellors to take responsibility for their lives. Furthermore, counsellors may put themselves in spurious positions of expertness and then not be able to 'deliver the goods'.

If you ask too many questions then the client will expect solutions just like s/he gets when s/he goes to his GP.

If you are going to ask questions in counselling then here are some tips that will help you:

- Don't set up a question and answer pattern in your relationship with your client.

Introduction to Counselling Skills and Theory

- Avoid questions in the first few minutes of the first session.

- Think carefully before asking questions at all.

- Instead ask yourself "Why do I want to know this?"

- Will it really help the other person, or is it just getting me out of a sticky situation.

Too many questions

Here the client is likely to feel interrogated and on the defensive. For example: 'Did you talk to your friend? What did he say?' How did you react?' 'Why did you react that way?'

Closed questions

A distinction is sometimes made between open and closed questions. The closed question limits or closes the client's options for responding, whereas the open question leaves his or her options open. An example of a closed question is 'Do you want to come for counselling once a fortnight or not at all?', whereas an open question would be 'How do you feel about making future counselling appointments?

Leading questions

Introduction to Counselling Skills and Theory

Leading questions put pressure on the client to answer in a certain way. They are often the counsellors need rather than the client's. An example is 'Did you feel angry when she came round to see you?' as contrasted with the more open 'How do you feel when she came round to see you?' At worst, leading questions may be totally unrelated to the client's current train of thought or even to his or her concerns.

Poorly timed questions

Timing is critical in the asking of good questions. For instance, a girl may be full of emotion as she relates to having a row with her husband", when the counsellor says: "What was your contribution to causing the row?' It is conceivable that when she had calmed down the girl might have been willing to explore the adequacy of her own behaviour in the situation, possibly without prompting from the counsellor.

'Why' questions

The risk of ' why ' questions such as 'Why did you do it?' is that they lead to a search for intellectual explanations which are of little help to the counselling process.

It is often better for the counsellor to ask "how" questions, e.g. "How did you behave in that situation, if the client is to gain insight into his or her behaviour. For instance, a why question might be 'Why don't you get on well with

Introduction to Counselling Skills and Theory

your boyfriend?', whereas a how question would be "How do you behave when things aren't going well with your boyfriend?"

Questions that fit with the core conditions:

- Checking out questions:

    "Is that what you meant"

- Exploration questions:

    "Would you like to say more about that?"

- Repeating clients' questions:

    "Why did that have to happen to me?"

- Focusing questions:

    "I think it might help if we talk about one thing at a time, which would you like to talk about first?"

Don't use questions:

- To lead the other person to a conclusion that you have prepared.

- Too frequently

Introduction to Counselling Skills and Theory

- That limits the possible answers to yes or no.

- To take control of the session.

- To break into a silence.

- To rescue the client by diverting their attention away from a painful issue.

- To satisfy your curiosity or to be nosey.

Do use questions:

- To help people explore either old or new territory.

    "How do these experiences of rejection affect you"

- To help people elaborate their experience, or give more detail.

    "Would you like to talk more about that?"

- To help people move into feelings.

    "How do you feel right now?"

- To help someone bring into focus an experience on the edge of their awareness.

Introduction to Counselling Skills and Theory

"You mentioned your daughter fleetingly then, with a troubled look on your face. What feelings do you think you might have about her?"

- To help someone explore their fantasies or imaginations.

"What do you imagine might happen if your wife left you?"

Thoughts:

Monitor and explore your own ways of asking questions in helping situations.

Introduction to Counselling Skills and Theory

Chapter 10
Personal Development Tool

Johari Window

It is extremely important that you go on your own personal journey of self discovery when in training,

A way of doing this is to gain feedback from others on how you come across. Sometimes we are aware of our presentation to others and we may have some awareness of why we present in a certain way. However, we can be unaware of our presentation and wonder why we are treated in a certain way.

Think of the times when someone has said something to you and you have internalised this as criticism. It may well have been. However, it may have been the truth and feedback to grow, which you have discounted.

Introduction to Counselling Skills and Theory

Part of your training is trio work as described earlier in this book. It is important that after each role play the observer, and the client give the helper constructive feedback. It is also central to us getting into the practice of the time when we may need to give own clients feedback.

Good feedback is:

- Timely

- Individual

- Specific

- Balanced

- Focused on behaviour

- Comes from multiple perspectives

- Constructive

- Empowering

Using feedback:

- Review your feedback

Introduction to Counselling Skills and Theory

- What have you learnt?

- What will you do differently as a result?

- Remember it's one person's perspective

- Ask for clarification

- Ask for more specific feedback

- Get other perspectives

Uncomfortable feelings are often a gift, so take your feedback as encouragement to grow.

Remember self awareness is essential to counselling training and when you are practicing as a counsellor.

Therefore it is important that trainee counsellors go on this journey of self discovery so that firstly they can change some of the things that are happening to them, changing their own unhealthy behaviours.

Secondly they need to know how they may come across to clients, as this can have an impact on our developing a warm and trusting relationship.

Introduction to Counselling Skills and Theory

Thirdly, our clients may give us feedback and we need to be able to accept it graciously without becoming defensive.

This may be uncomfortable for you, but if we never got feedback, where would we be today. Think back on some of the times you received feedback.

- Was if effective

- Did it facilitate a change in you?

- Was it ineffective?

- What did you do with the ineffective feedback?

We can use a model called **Johari window** to get a better understanding of our self.

The Johari window model was created by Joseph Luft and Harry Ingram to help us to understand our self awareness.

The Johari window is also referred to as:

- A disclosure feedback model of self awareness

- An information processing model

Introduction to Counselling Skills and Theory

- A personal development tool

- A tool to improve communications

- A tool to improve interpersonal relationships

- A tool to improve group dynamics

- A tool for team development and intergroup relationships

If one person calls you a horse, **IGNORE THEM**.

If three people call you a horse, **LOOK IN THE MIRROR**

If five people call you a horse, **BUY A SADDLE!**

If there are enough people telling you something you may want to listen to them!

Introduction to Counselling Skills and Theory

Johari Window model

Within the Johari window model there are four panes as follows:

	KNOWN BY SELF	**UNKNOWN BY SELF**
KNOWN BY OTHERS	**Open/free area** Things that you and other people know about	**Blind area** Things that you are not aware of but other people see
UNKNOWN BY OTHERS	**Hidden area** Things that you know about self but others don't	**Unknown area** Things that you and others do not know

Introduction to Counselling Skills and Theory

Your personal window

OPEN **KNOWN BY SELF AND KNOWN BY OTHERS**	BLIND **UNKOWN BY SELF KNOWN BY OTHERS**
HIDDEN **KNOWN BY SELF AND UNKNOWN TO OTHERS**	UNKNOWN AREA **UNKNONW BY SELF AND UNKNOWN BY OTHERS**

Introduction to Counselling Skills and Theory

Name:

Date:

ABLE	DEPENDABLE	INTELLIGENT	PATIENT	SENSIBLE
REFLECTIVE	DIGNIFIED	INTROVERTED	POWERFUL	SENTIMENTAL
ADAPTABLE	ENERGETIC	KIND	PROUD	SHY
BOLD	EXTROVERTED	INTERESTING	QUIET	SILLY
BRAVE	FRIENDLY	LOGICAL	ACCEPTING	SMART
CALM	GIVING	LOVING	RELAXED	SPONTANEOUS
CARING	HAPPY	MATURE	HONEST	SYMPATHETIC
CHEERFUL	HELPFUL	MODEST	RESPONSIVE	LAID BACK
CLEVER	EMPATHIC	SPIRITUAL	SEARCHING	TRUSTWORTHY
NON JUDGEMENTAL	INDEPENDENCE	OBSERVANT	ASSERTIVE	WARM
CONFIDENT	INGENIOUS	ORGANISED	WITTY	OPEN

Introduction to Counselling Skills and Theory

1. Put a tick in the boxes of the five characteristics that represent you from this list, and put them in your open box on your Johari window.

2. Pass this around to your peers and ask them to put a tick in the box of a characteristic that best suits you. Now build your own simple Johari window as follows:

    - Categorise as "OPEN" all the traits that at least one other person identified that you identified
    - Categorise as "BLIND" all traits that others have listed and you did not
    - Categorise as "HIDDEN" all traits you listed that others did not list
    - Categorise the rest of the traits in "UNKNOWN"

NOW THAT WE HAVE EXAMINED THE GOOD, LETS TAKE A LOOK AT THE BAD AND THE UGLY!

The Johari window can also be used as a tool to examine unknown areas that need to be developed.

Do the same with this list of characters and **remember it is not criticism it is feedback to grow!**

Introduction to Counselling Skills and Theory

BLASÉ	DISTANT	INANE	NEEDY	TIMID
BOASTFUL	DISPASSIONATE	INATTENTIVE	PUSHY	UNETHICAL
BRASH	DULL	INCOMPETENT	DRAMATIC	UNHAPPY
IRRITABLE	EMBARRASSED	INFLEXIBLE	PANICKY	UNHELPFUL
CHAOTIC	FOOLISH	INSECURE	PASSIVE	UNIMAGINATIVE
CHILDISH	GLUM	INSENSITIVE	PREDICTABLE	UNRELIABLE
COLD	HOSTILE	INTOLERANT	RASH	NEEDY
COWARD	HUMOURLESS	IRRATIONAL	SELFISH	VIOLENT
CREEPY	IGNORANT	IRRESPONSIBLE	SELF SATISFIED	IGNORANT
SLY	IMPATIENT	LETHARGIC	SMUG	WEAK
CYNICAL	IMPERCEPTIVE	LOUD	WITHDRAWN	AGGRESSIVE

Remember this is only people's perceptions of you. It may not be who you are, it may be down to the way that you present. Don't run away from feedback it can help you to develop as a person as well as a counsellor

Introduction to Counselling Skills and Theory

Chapter 11

Hunches & Immediacy

Sometimes we may have a hunch, a feeling in our stomach (hunches very rarely come from the mind). Our client may say something and all of a sudden we get a feeling in our stomach or for some the chest. It is really important to listen to this because it is our intuition and is very often important to the therapeutic process.

If appropriate share it with the client because very rarely are your hunches totally wrong.

If the client disagrees, that is okay stay with that as s/he may not be ready to explore this at that moment in time, or of course our hunches are not always right.

Rogers stuck, rigidly to the core conditions, however **Robert Carkhuff** developed another condition needed in the therapeutic relationship it was:

Introduction to Counselling Skills and Theory

- Immediacy

Immediacy is about what is going on in the room between therapist and client. It is a sort of challenge without being too confrontational that moves the client on to insight.

The definition of immediacy is the ability of the counsellor to use the immediate situation to invite the client to look at what is going on between them in the relationship.

It often feels risky and unfamiliar. It involves sharing a bit of you. It implies the use of the present tense. It is one of the most powerful skills in counselling.

In its fullest use, immediacy involves the following:

Revealing how you are feeling/thinking/sensing.

Sharing a hunch or sense of what the client may be feeling/thinking/sensing in the here and now (and possibly linking this to the client's issue).

Inviting the client to explore what is going on between the two of you.

For example:

"I notice that you haven't engaged with me all session, which is leaving me feeling rather shut out. It feels as if

Introduction to Counselling Skills and Theory

you want to stop me getting too close ... Is that how it feels to you?"

It is always helpful to have an idea on when it is appropriate to use immediacy in the therapeutic relationship.

Here are some tips:

1. To address (in order to help the client understand it better/deal with it) any explicit or implicit pattern of relating (of the client's) that may be being repeated in the helping relationship.

Examples:

"I notice that you are responding very defensively to what I am saying. I feel very accepting of what you are telling me. But I sense that you feel that I am judging you. I wonder whether this is because.................

"I am aware that you have said that you never get angry, yet I am sensing that you are very angry with me even though you are not expressing that anger."

2. To deal with difficulties, within the relationships for example:

    (a) Lack of trust:

Introduction to Counselling Skills and Theory

"You told me in our first session that you have never trusted anyone in your life and that you find it difficult to trust.

I wonder whether this is affecting how you feel towards me because I am sensing that you are not finding it easy to trust me.

Is that how may be feeling to you?"

(b) Boundary issues:

"I am finding it difficult to concentrate on what you are saying because I have just realised that I know the person you are talking about ... I am wondering whether you have notice my reaction and this is somehow affecting your ability to talk freely."

(c) An issue of difference that might be affecting the relationship:

"I am aware that you are a gay female and I am a heterosexual male and I wonder how easy you are finding it to tell me about your experience of sexual discrimination at work. Can we talk about this?"

Guidelines for using immediacy as the counsellor/helper:

Be direct clear and honest about your own internal response.

Introduction to Counselling Skills and Theory

Be sensitive to the client, being aware of what is difficult and choosing your words carefully.

Be very aware of timing and the possible impact of this intervention.

Check out who it is for: "Why am I saying this? Will it help my client?"

Be prepared to take the risk and follow through whatever emerges.

Some phrases that you might find helpful when exploring your client's world, feelings, behaviours and thoughts are:

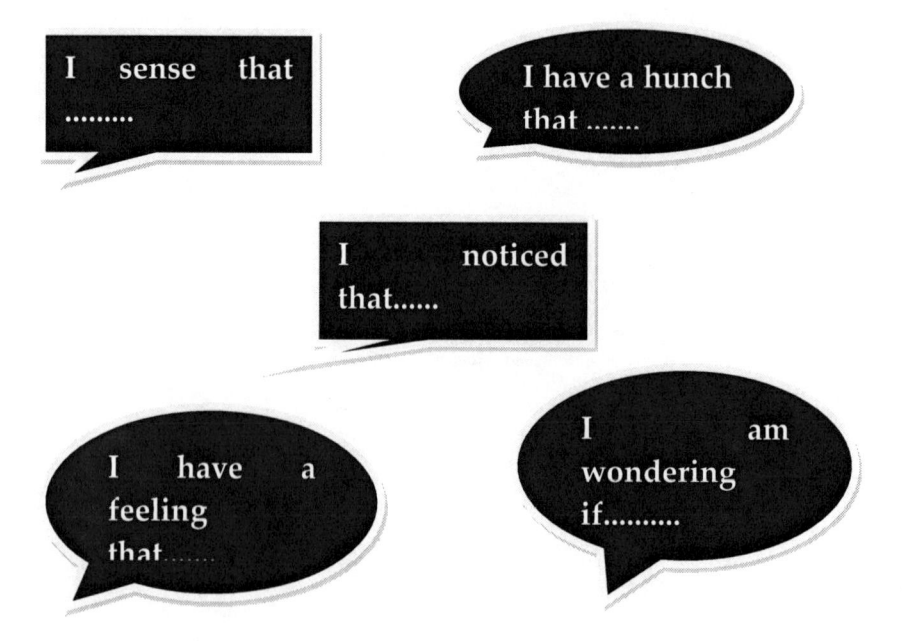

- I sense that..........
- I have a hunch that.......
- I noticed that......
- I have a feeling that........
- I am wondering if..........

Introduction to Counselling Skills and Theory

It is very much about using what is happening in the therapy room. What is happening in the relationship between you and the client? Often client's will behave in the same way with you as they do with significant others in their lives, therefore this enables you to see how their way of relating may be impacting on others and subsequently be creating the problems that they are experiencing. It is about being congruent within the therapeutic relationship.

An example of this from my own practice is a client I was working with talked non-stop in all our sessions. He controlled the conversation and left very little room for any interventions from me. He was presenting with relationship difficulties. His wife was suffering with depression and spent most of the time in bed leaving him doing all the chores and the taking care of the children.

I only had twelve sessions with him so I asked him on our fourth session what he was getting out of counselling. He replied that it was somewhere in which he could offload to enable him to get through the following week. This was all well and good but I wondered what he was going to do with this load that he was dumping when the therapy was over.

On our fifth session as usual he talked and talked and talked and I remember thinking "Oh God, I wish that I hadn't got out of bed this morning." Ping! Now I knew why his wife did not get out of bed.

Introduction to Counselling Skills and Theory

Obviously, I was not going to tell him my thoughts, but what I did say was "I am noticing in our sessions that you do all the talking and it is very difficult for me to offer any interventions that may be able to help you." I let him sit in silence and process this then said. "I sense that this might be how your wife may be feeling, perhaps unheard." The client took this on board and recognised that this might be a barrier to his wife's recovery.

From this we went on to look at improving his listening skills so that he could try these at home. Things improved, his wife got up out of bed and began helping him with the chores, she accessed help herself for her depression and things improved for my client.

This is an example of how being congruent and using immediacy can work. However please me mindful of the guidelines in this chapter because if you are not then the risk is that your client may jump out of the chair and never come back.

> **Thoughts:**
>
> What would you do if you used this skill and the client became defensive?
>
> How might you continue to promote a warm empathic relationship?

Introduction to Counselling Skills and Theory

Chapter 12
Ambivalence

Ambivalence is a normal aspect of human nature. Passing through ambivalence is a natural phase in the process of change.

It is when people get stuck in ambivalence that problems can persist and intensify.

| **"I WANT TO AND I DON'T WANT TO"** |

Ambivalence is a reasonable place to be but you wouldn't want to live there! It can be uncomfortable but again be mindful to recognise that it is also normal.

You may want to normalise this with your client too. Show the client acceptance for where s/he is in their process.

Introduction to Counselling Skills and Theory

To explore ambivalence is to work at the heart of the problem of being stuck. Until a person can resolve the "I want to, but I don't want to" dilemma, change is likely to be slow-going and short lived.

Ambivalent people appear to lack motivation and may not respond in a logical manner.

The question to ask is not "Why isn't this person motivated?" but rather "For what is this person motivated?"

It is the client's task, not the counsellor's to articulate and resolve his or her ambivalence.

Direct persuasion is not an effective method for resolving ambivalence.

It is important that we help the client explore their ambivalence. Staying with the clients process. To do this we need to:

Introduction to Counselling Skills and Theory

- Seek to understand the person's frame of reference, particularly via reflective listening. (Advanced empathy)

- Express acceptance and affirmation

- Elicit and selectively reinforcing the clients own self motivational statements expressions of problem recognition, concern, desire and intention to change, and ability to change.

- Monitor the client's degree of readiness to change, and ensure that resistance is not generated by jumping ahead of client.

- Affirm the client's freedom of choice and self direction.

*Stay with the stuckness, **don't** try to resolve it!*

Introduction to Counselling Skills and Theory

The counsellor needs to remain a friendly consultant, never criticizing the client's effort or difficulties, always attempting to provide empathy and support, yet also willing and able to provide feedback and helpful suggestions to the client as the client becomes ready to consider them.

SOME TIPS:

- Empathise with difficulty of ambivalence

- Ask if there is something else which would help to make a decision

- Ask if they have a plan to manage not making a decision.

- Ask if they are interested in reducing some of the problems (restate problems) while they are trying to make a decision.

RECOGNISING AMBIVALENCE:

- ✓ Client who misses lots of appointments

- ✓ Client who appears defensive

- ✓ Client who appears to lack motivation

- ✓ Client who discusses reasons for not changing

Introduction to Counselling Skills and Theory

- ✓ Indecisiveness and hesitancy

- ✓ Resistance

It is also important to remember that even when a client appears to have made a decision and is taking steps to change, ambivalence is still likely to be present.

> **Thoughts:**
>
> How comfortable are you with ambivalence?
>
> How may you improve your ability to stay with the client's ambivalence?

Introduction to Counselling Skills and Theory

Chapter 13
Self disclosure

Self disclosure is the process of revealing more about ourselves to others either consciously or unconsciously.

Self disclosure can be about what the client discloses to us or what we can disclose to them. In this chapter we will be looking at the later.

What we need to be looking at as trainee counsellors is:

How appropriate is it in the helping profession?

When is it okay to disclose, when is it not?

Is it okay to say "I have been through that problem and this is what I did"

If not why not?

Introduction to Counselling Skills and Theory

There are different schools of thought in relation to whether a counsellor can or should disclose personal information about themselves to clients.

Psychodynamic theorists would say that there should be no disclosure whatsoever, and many that practice this model would not tell a client anything about their professional or personal life.

Other theorists believe that not to show a little of ourselves to clients could impact on the relationship in the following ways:

- Clients may see the therapist as the expert that is going to 'fix' them.

- Clients could be wary about disclosing to the therapist.

- It could create an unequal relationship.

- Therapist may be seen as incongruent.

- Clients could feel rejected.

Rule of thumb:

The main thing to consider when thinking about your own practice is, if you are going to disclose something about 'you' to the client then it should only be when it

Introduction to Counselling Skills and Theory

benefits the client – not when it benefits you. As a counsellor or helper which of these issues might you disclose and which would you definitely not disclose?

Would you disclose the following:	Yes or no	Why?
1. I'm going on holiday next week so will need to book you in the week after.		
2. I smoked cannabis when I was about 16		
3. My husband works at the same place as you do		
4. My daughter has just fell out with her boyfriend		
5. I used to do the same and this is how I dealt with this problem		
6. I am leaving in a month's time as I've been offered a better opportunity		
7. I am going to party this weekend		
8. I am a little unwell and so may have to cut our session short		
9. I have four children their names are........		
10. I have been married three		

Introduction to Counselling Skills and Theory

times so I know all about relationships		
11. I know the person that you are talking about		

Once you have answered these questions you may need to think about the following answers:

1. A client does need to know that you are unable to see them the following week, but do they need to know why?

2. No a client does not need to know this even if you are working with substance misuse services. A good answer to give if you are asked is "Why is it important for you to know this?"

3. I would guess that most of you will have answered no to this, but take this into consideration what if your client sees his counsellor and work colleague hand in hand in town? What might he think?

4. No a client does not need to know this.

5. No, we all have unique personalities and histories, just because your solution worked for you does not mean it will work for the client. This is not empowering them to find their own solution.

125

Introduction to Counselling Skills and Theory

6. A client does need to know if you are leaving the organisation but do they need to know why?

7. No, this is not appropriate.

8. Would you continue to work while feeling too unwell to practice? Would you be working when you feel 'unfit to practice'?

9. No.

10. No

11. Yes, it would be unethical to continuing to work with this client as there could be a conflict of interest.

> **Thoughts:**
>
> What are your thoughts on self disclosure, no disclosure or some?
>
> Imagine yourself in the client's shoes, what might it be like for him or her if there is no disclosure or some?
>
> Does some disclosure enhance the relationship as some theorists believe?

Introduction to Counselling Skills and Theory

**Chapter 14
Helping versus enabling**

One of the things to be mindful of, and from my experience is a common problem within counselling training, is not to try to fix the client. It is about in a sense empowering the client to find the solution to their own problem.

When in training you are learning a lot of theories and can become over keen to try out these theoretical models.

Theories are there prominently to help you to understand human psychopathology, NOT for you to make a diagnosis and then try to cure.

I hear a lot of students say "I am comfortable with initiating a therapeutic relationship and with facilitating a safe ending but I don't know what to do in the middle. This is because they see this as the 'fixing' stage.

Introduction to Counselling Skills and Theory

The short answer is nothing, Stay with the relationship. Use the theory to help you to understand your client and enable you to step into their world.

It is about helping the client not enabling or caring for and not rescuing

HELPING is doing something for someone that he is not capable of doing himself.

ENABLING is doing for someone what he could and should be doing for himself. Enabling creates an atmosphere in which the people that we care for can comfortably continue their unacceptable behaviour.

Likewise there is a difference between 'caring' for someone and 'rescuing' someone.

CARING is empathising with the client and their problem and giving them the space to talk about the issue and empowering them to find their own solution to their own problem.

RESCUING is advice giving, solving the problem for them or 'doing' for them. This is disempowering the client from 'doing' for himself.

Here is a model for learning the difference between caring and rescuing which comes from Transactional Analysis.

Introduction to Counselling Skills and Theory

The Drama/Winners Triangle

THE DRAMA TRIANGLE

PERSECUTOR

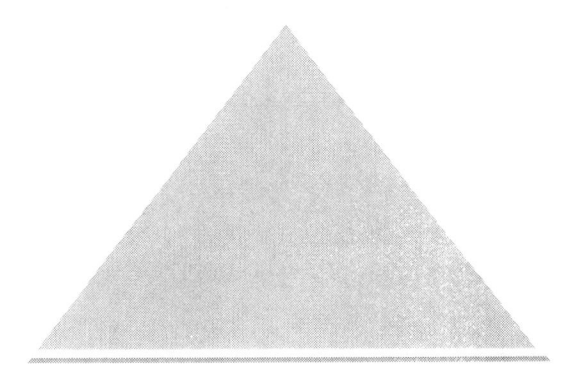

RESCUER   **VICTIM**

The drama triangle is the unhealthy triangle.

When people come to us with problems they are often in the 'victim' position and we can automatically go into rescuing.

We rescue for lots of different reasons. For example:

- **The pay off:-** For a reward, to raise our own self esteem or so that they will be there for us when we have a problem.

- **To get rid of:-** To sort out there problem so that they won't come back to us with the same issue, to

Introduction to Counselling Skills and Theory

allow us to get on with our own life/day/jobs, so they don't take up too much of our time/energy.

- **To feel needed:-** Some of us have a need to be needed and if we don't can feel lonely.

- **To help us:-** To avoid what is going on in our own lives and the uncomfortable thoughts and feelings associated with this.

There is room for a shift on this triangle. For example rescuing can lead to a shift to 'persecutor' when:

- We feel that our advice has not been listened to.

- We have spent the whole day with them, neglecting our own duties and they have not taken our advice.

- We have sorted out their problem and they have still gone back to the same situation.

We may then move to the **'victim'** because:

- We feel hurt that they haven't taken our advice/gone back to the same situation

- We feel hurt because we have had a fight with them about ignoring our advice or using up our time and energy and made no change.

Introduction to Counselling Skills and Theory

WHEN WE RESCUE PEOPLE WE DISEMPOWER THEM, WE TAKE AWAY THEIR OWN RESOURCES TO 'THINK, FEEL AND DO' FOR THEMSELVES.

However, on the:

WINNERS TRIANGLE

ASSERTIVE

CARER **VULNERABLE**

There is no shift. This is the healthy triangle.

➢ A friend or family member comes to you with a problem, you know that this friend might not take your advice and may spend the whole day complaining about their problem or the person that they perceive caused the problem.

Introduction to Counselling Skills and Theory

- You say "Gosh, I can see you are really upset" or "Gosh, that sounds painful" or any empathic response of your choice. Then you say "I can give you an hour to talk about this, but you know anything that can't be sorted in an hour cannot usually be sorted that day." So straight away you are taking care of **Your** time and psychological energy.

- When they have told you their 'story' you then say words to the effect of "What are you going to do about that, and "how can I support you in your decision" – (needless to say we all communicate differently, so you may find a way to say this in a dissimilar way, however meaning the same).

- This way, you have:

    - Not jumped into advice giving or running around rescuing.

    - Not used up too much of your time and energy but still been caring and supportive.

    - Not held any resentments, anger or hurt because you have given advice or run around rescuing, and the person has not taken your advice.

Introduction to Counselling Skills and Theory

- If they have gone back to the same situation, then it is easier to accept as their choice.

And last but not least:

EMPOWERED THIS PERSON TO THINK, FEEL AND DO FOR THEMSELVES.

> **Thoughts:**
>
> Can you recall times in your own life when you have rescued someone?
>
> What was the outcome?
>
> How did you feel afterwards?
>
> Is this model something that you can use in your own personal life?

Introduction to Counselling Skills and Theory

**Chapter 15
Personal development
Prejudice & oppression in the helping relationship**

Prejudice:

Prejudice in the helping profession is not just about being judgemental to people that are a different colour, religion, and sexual orientation than us.

We are all becoming increasingly more aware of the prejudice in these areas within society today. However have you thought about the prejudice that you may hold against certain types of people. Their characteristics, the way they behave, their way of thinking or feeling?

Prejudice can include being judgemental about difference too, the different way that people think, feel and behave.

For example:

Introduction to Counselling Skills and Theory

How do you feel about the following types of people?

- People who sulk
- People who think negatively
- Opinionated people
- Highly emotional people
- People who act tough
- People who make a joke out of everything
- People who use drugs or alcohol
- People who gamble
- People who have affairs
- People who pretend to know it all
- People who judge others
- People that rescue others
- Dramatic people
- Quiet People

Introduction to Counselling Skills and Theory

- Loud people

- People who keep their distance

- People who suck up to others

- People who play the victim

And so on and so on.

How are you able to offer the core conditions to the person on this list that you struggle with, or indeed maybe one that is not listed?

Have a think about the types of people that you struggle to relate with.

Now think about the following:

- How might you be able to work with this type of person?

- What may you have to do to enable you to develop empathy for a client with this character style, way of thinking, feeling or behaving?

As a trainee counsellor this is the type of self exploration that you will need to do to enable you to practice safely and to enable you to develop a warm and empathic relationship with others.

Introduction to Counselling Skills and Theory

Oppression/power:

Where do we sit in terms of the following question:

Should the counsellor/helper be equal to the client to enable them to develop a therapeutic alliance?

What are your thoughts?

Spend some time thinking about this.

It would be ideal if we could develop an equal relationship with our clients however there is an inequality.......................... They are asking for help.

The client may:

- Be uncomfortable about asking for help unless the helper is equal

    OR
- Be uncomfortable about asking for help unless the helper is an expert and will give them full quality of help.

So as counsellors how might we be able to offer the above to our clients?

The important thing is:

- To share your expertise in a non oppressive way

Introduction to Counselling Skills and Theory

- Be human and not robotic

- Be fair and mindful of the clients characteristics/personality

- Be understanding and respectful

> In a setting such as this we should all be allowed to make mistakes.

Ooops! In a setting such as this we should all be allowed to make mistakes.

Thoughts:

Explore your own prejudices, and how you might overcome them.

Introduction to Counselling Skills and Theory

Chapter 16
Advanced Empathy

We have talked earlier in the book about one of Carl Rogers core conditions 'empathy' and how this is about being able to step into the clients shoes and feel what they are feeling.

In this chapter we are going to discuss advanced empathy. Advanced empathy is being able to step into a client's internal frame of reference and to be able to get a sense of the client's deeper feelings, feelings that they may not be expressing in words.

To explain advanced empathy I first need to explain a little about how we as human beings function (internal & external frame of reference) and how experiences as children may teach us to hide what we are really feeling.

Internal & External frame of reference.

Introduction to Counselling Skills and Theory

Firstly we need to be able to look at the client's world from their point of view.

The client's inner world includes:

- Cultural influences
- Beliefs and values
- Memories
- Feelings, thoughts and emotions
- Behaviours
- Experiences
- Sensations & perceptions
- Meanings

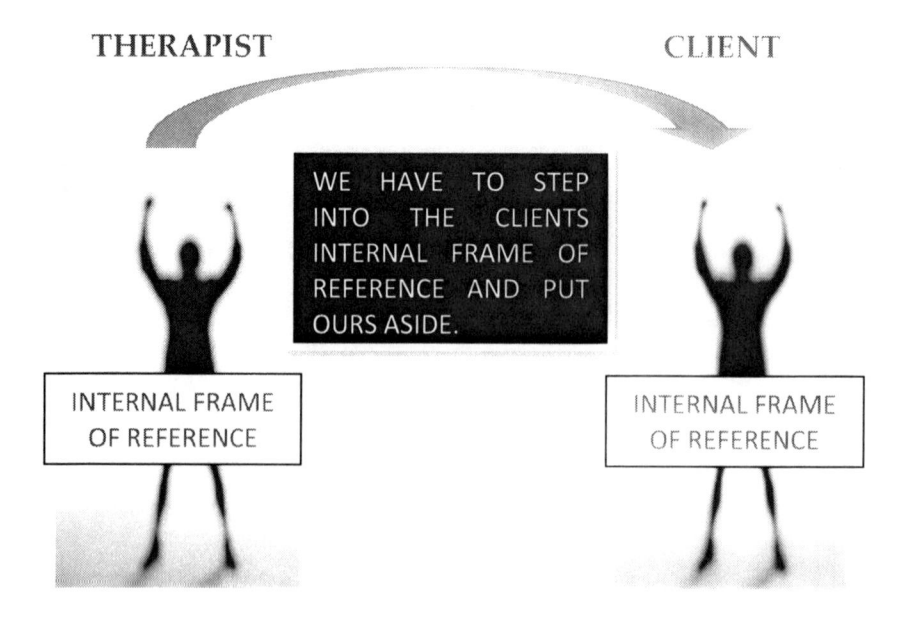

THERAPIST **CLIENT**

WE HAVE TO STEP INTO THE CLIENTS INTERNAL FRAME OF REFERENCE AND PUT OURS ASIDE.

INTERNAL FRAME OF REFERENCE

INTERNAL FRAME OF REFERENCE

Introduction to Counselling Skills and Theory

To do this we have to consider the uniqueness of each person's frame of reference in that moment of time. They may be sat in the same environment as you, at the same moment, but the way they experience that moment is seen through their unique frame of reference. If we interpret their story through our own internal frame of reference we will form judgements or offer advice.

We can't really put our own frame of reference completely aside, but we can become aware of it enough to recognise what is our stuff (our internal frame of reference) and treat it as such. If we are unable to do this then we are unable to offer the client the core conditions.

This is another reason that we need personal development as part of our counselling training. Take the example of self harming.

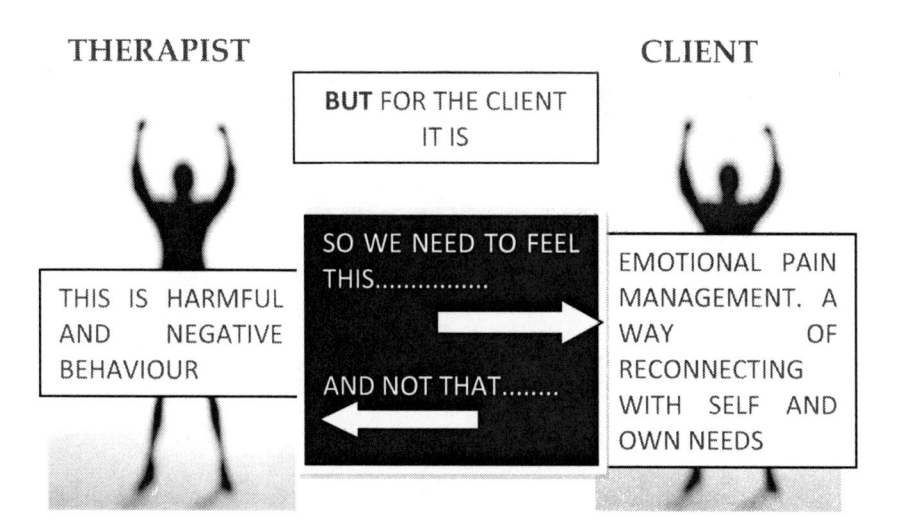

THERAPIST   **CLIENT**

BUT FOR THE CLIENT IT IS

THIS IS HARMFUL AND NEGATIVE BEHAVIOUR

SO WE NEED TO FEEL THIS..............

AND NOT THAT........

EMOTIONAL PAIN MANAGEMENT. A WAY OF RECONNECTING WITH SELF AND OWN NEEDS

Introduction to Counselling Skills and Theory

If I am stuck in my own frame of reference, I cannot hear the main points of someone else's frame of reference, nor comprehend their behaviour, all I can do is fail to understand and offer advice.

If I can recognise my own stuff and put it aside then I can begin to get a picture of the client's frame of reference – which will make the behaviour understandable and possibly logical.

Read the following story:

> **Woody Allen was married to Mia Farrow who brought into the relationship a number of natural and adopted children from previous relationships. One of which was his step daughter Soon-yi. As Soon-yi reached adulthood, she and Woody Allen decided to develop a new partnership. He divorced his wife and set up home with Soon-yi.**

What issues are there for you?

Now look at it from Woody Allen's frame of reference?

Now consider Soon-Yi's frame of reference?

Introduction to Counselling Skills and Theory

How do you see Woody and Mia based on their behaviour?

We also need to consider external frames of reference. These are outside influences that can prevent you from offering empathy to your clients:

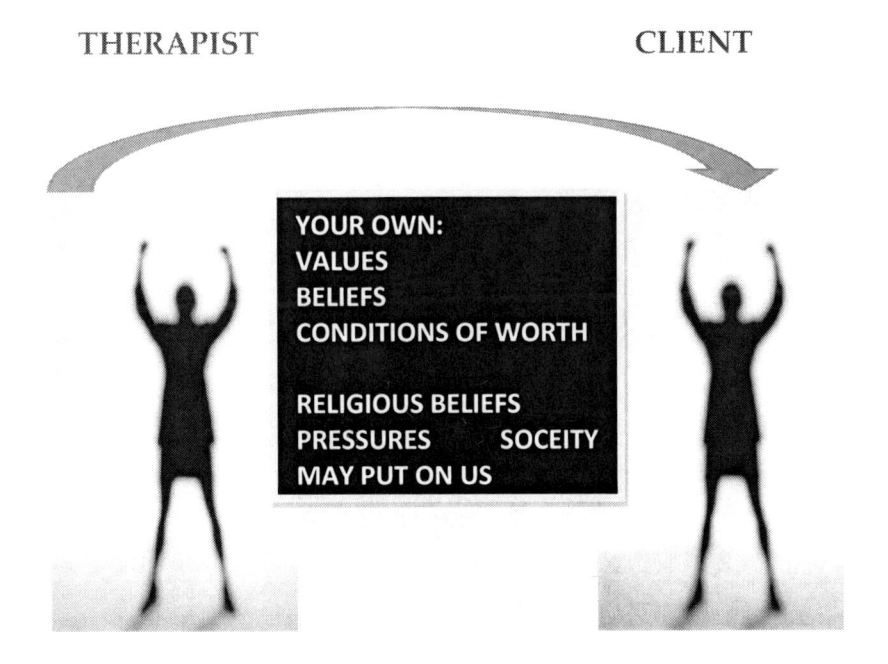

THERAPIST **CLIENT**

YOUR OWN:
VALUES
BELIEFS
CONDITIONS OF WORTH

RELIGIOUS BELIEFS
PRESSURES   SOCEITY
MAY PUT ON US

Read the following story:

> **If you knew a woman who was pregnant (a friend not a client) who had eight children already. Three who were deaf, two who were blind, one mentally retarded and she had syphilis. Would you recommend an abortion? BE HONEST!**

Introduction to Counselling Skills and Theory

If you answered yes.

CONGRATULATIONS YOU HAVE JUST KILLED BEETHOVEN!

Your answer may have come from either your internal or external frame of reference. So, to work ethically as a therapist you will need to learn to step into the client's internal frame of reference.

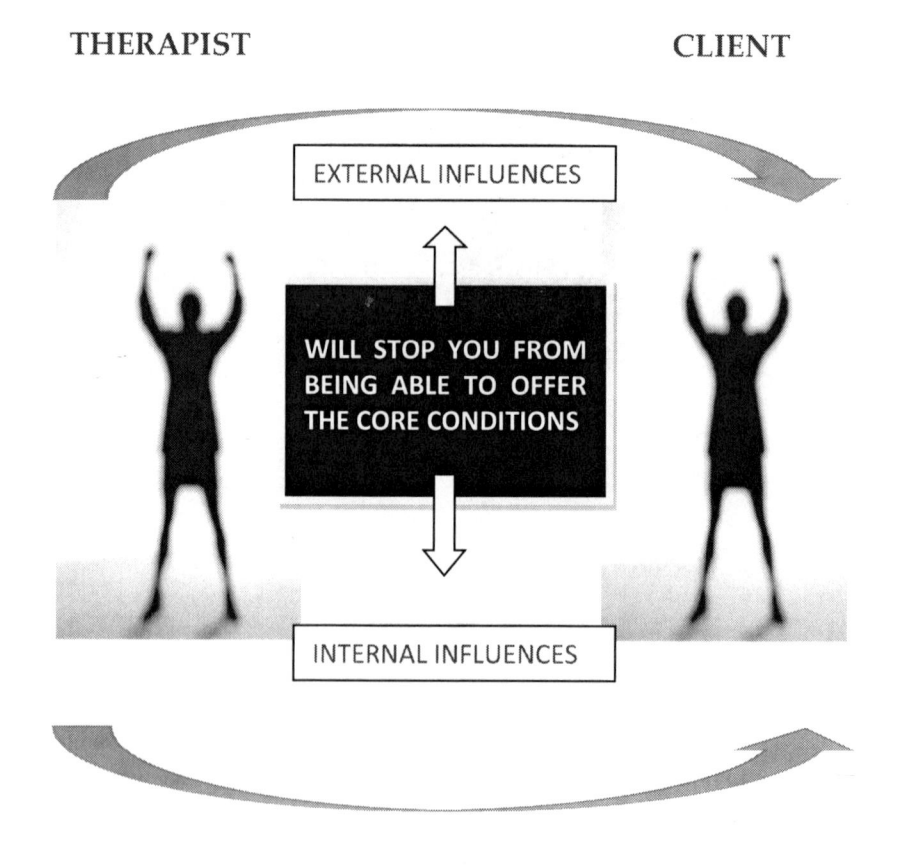

THERAPIST   **CLIENT**

EXTERNAL INFLUENCES

WILL STOP YOU FROM BEING ABLE TO OFFER THE CORE CONDITIONS

INTERNAL INFLUENCES

Introduction to Counselling Skills and Theory

Your external and internal frame of reference may also inhibit you from offering advanced empathy. Stepping into a clients frame of reference is offering your client advanced empathy.

Now we will look at 'feelings'.

Clients sometimes come into therapy and express non authentic feelings; these feelings replace feelings that are forbidden.

These are feelings that were discounted, not allowed, laughed at etc when we were younger. So we replaced them with what we learned were more acceptable feelings. Those are feelings which were deemed as acceptable in our world.

Eric Berne the founder of transactional analysis called these non authentic feelings "Racket feelings."

He states that:

"As young children, we may notice that in our family, certain feelings are encouraged, while others are prohibited. To get our love and attention we may decide to feel only the permitted feelings. This decision is made without conscious awareness. When we play out our script in grown up life, we continue to cover our authentic feelings with the feelings that were permitted to us as

Introduction to Counselling Skills and Theory

children. These substitute feelings are known as racket feelings."

By listening and learning from our client and using our skills such as reflection, paraphrasing and challenge. Also by stepping into our client's frame of reference, we may be able to offer advanced empathy.

Advanced empathy.

Advanced empathy is described as a reflection of content and feeling at a deeper level.

The purpose of advanced empathy is to try and get an understanding of what may be deeper feelings, feelings that the client may not be expressing.

For example:

"I get the sense that you are really angry about what was said, but I am wondering if you also feel a little hurt by it."

OR

"You said that you feel more confident about contacting your employers, but I wonder if you also still feel a bit scared."

Introduction to Counselling Skills and Theory

Advanced empathy is offering back unstated feelings which you are picking up from body language or voice tone. Listening and seeing something that is not openly said but is felt. Going with your hunches as described in a previous chapter.

To listen to what is not being said is to:

- Listen to their story

- Note the body language for non verbal clues. (It could be a person that is tapping his foot and saying "I'm very relaxed" (incongruence)
OR
The person who is telling you his story about his abusive life and his fist is clenched and he is saying I'm not angry

- Listen to the tone of voice

- Look at limb movement eg a clenched fist or a tapping foot.

- Look at posture eg is their head bowed

- Look at their face eg eye to eye contact'

- What are her eyes telling you?

Introduction to Counselling Skills and Theory

There are 'Ten Basic Emotions' to watch out for:

- ✓ Love - caring concern

- ✓ Happiness - joy excitement contentment

- ✓ Sadness - despair depression

- ✓ Jealousy - Envy resentment

- ✓ Anger - rage frustration

- ✓ Lust – desire

- ✓ Fear – anxiety

- ✓ Greed

- ✓ Rejection – hurt

- ✓ Disgust - Shame

Advanced empathy is an attempt by the counsellor to impart meaning to the client by presenting a hypothesis about relationships among his/her behaviours (thoughts, feelings, behaviours) or reasons for his/her behaviours.

Introduction to Counselling Skills and Theory

The goal is a new client understanding, a new perspective.

It should only be used when:

- ✓ Client is prepared and ready to receive it.

- ✓ Close to awareness.

- ✓ Confidence in counsellor's expertise and competence.

- ✓ Rapport established--counsellor has best interests at heart.

- ✓ Evidence gathered--counsellor understands.

- ✓ Anxiety not too high (or too low)--motivated to change.

- ✓ Therapist is prepared to give and support it.

- ✓ Reasonably certain of accuracy.

- ✓ Has adequate evidence to document. If client says "What makes you think that?"

- ✓ Dosage--not too many at once.

Introduction to Counselling Skills and Theory

- ✓ Time allowed to process - not near the end of session.

- ✓ Be tactful, caring, and respectful.

- ✓ Be tentative

- ✓ Using phrases such as "perhaps", "sounds like", "could be"

- ✓ Be concise, but specific and clear.

Advanced empathy is much more powerful than basic empathy, as your client may not be consciously aware of these feelings. It is therefore best used tentatively and within a more established relationship.

Advanced empathy can often deepen your relationship with the client to facilitate change.

Thoughts:

Explore your own belief and value system.

Explore any unauthentic feelings that you may have, what are the feelings that you are not able to express and why?

Introduction to Counselling Skills and Theory

Chapter 17
Listening to and exploring the feeling content & identifying themes

The feeling content

Listening to a person's thought process is quite comfortable but some people become uncomfortable when listening to peoples feeling content. British culture can be quite rigid and limited in the way that we deal with the expression of feelings.

If we have a problem expressing feelings ourselves then we are likely to have problems being around when strong feelings are expressed. This will limit us and cramp our ability to genuinely listen to a wide range of feelings with respect.

As therapists we may say "Tell me how you feel." We need to be comfortable listening to how the client feels when asking that question.

Introduction to Counselling Skills and Theory

How do you feel to the following statements?

"After they told me that my mum was dead I walked back from the hospital in a daze. I walked over three miles, and I don't remember it at all. I was now a forty five year old orphan all alone in the world. I cried all the way home."

"If they expect more out of me at work then they can just go take a run and jump! They had better think again before abusing me! They put on me and put on me and I feel like punching them in the face!"

"Nobody takes me seriously. I always seem to be the butt of everyone's jokes. Everyone takes the mickey out of me. I feel like I am a worthless piece of manure"

"Nothing seems worth struggling for anymore. (......... Sob) I just don't think I can make it, just don't want to go on. My life is worthless; there is no point in being here. I feel hopeless."

What emotions do those clients stir up in you?

By being empathic we are trying to enter the client's world as completely as possible. It is not enough to recognise and name a feeling. Feelings come in different shapes and sizes.

Introduction to Counselling Skills and Theory

It would not be enough to say to the woman who's mum had died "So you felt sad and upset when your mum died" As it no way captures the depth and breadth of her experience.

It may not be enough to say to the client who is angry with his work "So you are feeling angry" if he is feeling rage.

As counsellors we need to develop a huge feeling vocabulary. This feeling grid may help you to develop a wider feeling vocabulary and can also help clients to express how they are feeling too. See how many feeling words that you can add to it.

SAD	MAD	GLAD	BAD	SCARED
Tearful	Angry	Happy	Naughty	Anxious
Unhappy	Furious	Elated	Rebellious	Frightened
Depressed	Outraged	Wonderful	Worthless	Petrified
Miserable	Livid	Ecstatic	Selfish	Mortified
Lonely	Hostile	Pleased	Bored	Helpless
Ashamed	Hateful	Joyful	Guilty	Submissive
Hurt	Rage	Content	Stupid	Insecure
Bashful	Frustrated	Excited	Daring	Inferior
Inadequate	Irritated	Energetic	Foolish	Embarrassed
Pensive	Bewildered	Proud	Jealous	Discouraged

It is not only the choice of words that we use which indicates the depth and breadth of feelings.

Introduction to Counselling Skills and Theory

It's also the way we say them! The dramatic effect when we use the words, how we emphasize the words, raise or lower the tone and volume of our voice.

Skilled use of summarising & reflection involves the use of a wide range of expression.

In your daily life, when listening to someone's problems try focusing exclusively on the feeling content of their world. You could try ignoring the rest of the storyline, just reflecting the feelings.

Identifying themes

Sometimes a client may be so embroiled in their problems they are unable to see the wood for the trees. They cannot find a solution to their problem, which is often why they are coming to you. The therapist on the other hand is able to get a wider view and take the time to do two important things:

- ✓ See patterns and themes in what the client is saying and doing.

- ✓ Make links or connections between thoughts, feelings, behaviours or events in the client's world.

The person coming to you for help is far too busy just coping and living with the problem to do either of those activities in a systemic way.

Introduction to Counselling Skills and Theory

If you see patterns and themes in the client's world, firstly check that it is not from your own view of the problem (frame of reference). Or an attempt to find a solution to the client problem (fix them).

Then present what you see to the client. Bear in mind you could be wrong and be mindful that the client may not be ready to hear it. Both are okay. Don't push it.

You could say something like:

"How does this sound to you?"

"This may ring bells for you if not ignore it."

Don't present your ideas as a scientific hypothesis; say it is your view.

"I think I have noticed a pattern"

"There may be a link here, let me explain so that you can judge for yourself"

Make a clear simple statement, don't make it sound complicated. Do not insist that you are right. Let go if your client can't see it. They may think about it and come back next week and see things differently. They may not.

Always be mindful that they may not be ready OR you may be wrong.

Introduction to Counselling Skills and Theory

> **Thoughts:**
>
> Can you see any patterns or themes in your own life?
>
> What are they?
>
> What impact are they having on your behaviour/life?

Introduction to Counselling Skills and Theory

Chapter 18
Different perspectives

When we are counselling we need to be able to see things from different perspectives and help our clients see things from a different perspective too. Clients often come in seeing their problem from one perspective.

A candle stick? Or two faces?

Introduction to Counselling Skills and Theory

This picture is a clear demonstration that things are often not as they seem, and there's almost always a different perspective. Some people will see two candlesticks, others will see two faces. It is the same with how people see their problems or indeed their lives.

When there's a traffic accident, police ask for witnesses to come forward to describe what happened. They like to have as many witness statements as possible, so they can build up a broader picture and a more realistic version of events.

In a traffic accident, there will be many different perspectives on what happened. The driver will have one perspective, another driver, or a passenger will have yet another perspective.

Each onlooker who witnessed the accident will have a slightly different perspective, depending on where they were, how far away they were, how much their view or vision was restricted, how much danger they felt they were in, what else was going on, how the accident affected them, what the accident means to them.

It is similar for therapists who do critical incident counselling after a major incident.

All the people involved in the incident will have different thoughts about the occurrence, different feelings and will

Introduction to Counselling Skills and Theory

have performed diverse actions. They will have all seen things from their individual viewpoint.

So it's the same principle with everything – each situation, event, conversation means something different to all those involved, and to those not involved. We give different meanings, according to our belief systems, and how we are affected by the event. We all have our own realities.

Anais Nin said: *"We don't see things as they are; we see things as we are"*

She meant by this that we see things from our own clouded perception of the world due to our own experiences and childhood messages.

In a critical incident for example one man may run around trying to rescue everyone because his belief is that this is the 'role' of a man, this is his belief system. The other may 'run for his life' because his belief system is that he must get more professional help. Neither is wrong and we should not judge either. Both these men acted on their own belief system when action was needed.

We look at situations, events, and interpret what other people say and do, according to our own set of past experiences, culture, faith, values, all of which help us form our beliefs about ourselves, about others, and about the world in general. The meaning we give events, the

Introduction to Counselling Skills and Theory

way we make sense of our world, is based upon our core belief system.

Our minds are constantly trying to make sense of our world, forming judgements and opinions about every situation, event, and interaction. Those judgements and opinions will be affected by our central or core belief system. It is as though we are looking at the world through distorted or coloured lenses – and everyone has their own personal prescription or colour for their glasses.

Our core belief system comprises of:

- How I think about myself
- Past experiences
- How I think about others

Our core belief system is formed and influenced by:

- Childhood upbringing
- How I think about the world
- Culture
- Faith
- Values
- Current circumstances
- Character, traits, including genetic influences

Here is an example of how our core belief system influences us:

Introduction to Counselling Skills and Theory

Childhood Experience
Bullied and hurt by others

Core beliefs
Others will hurt me
The world is a dangerous place
I am useless and unlovable
I must try to please others so that they like me and won't hurt me

New situations or events:
Sees situations & events as threatening & dangerous. Interprets others words & reactions as critical & threatening.

LENS: DISTORTED PERCEPTION

Introduction to Counselling Skills and Theory

This may lead to the following for this person:

Behaviour: Passive, goes along with what others want, doesn't talk much and avoids eye contact.

Emotions: Anxious, depressed, low self esteem

Thoughts: I'm vulnerable, this is dangerous, and I'm going to get hurt. I am useless and stupid. No-one likes me.

In this example, even situations which others find enjoyable and relaxing, this particular person will experience it very differently, and feel threatened by others.

A look, word or gesture intended to be friendly and kind, may be interpreted as "They don't mean that. They're only trying to be kind to me because they pity me". Or even, "They mean to hurt me".

Their mind is interpreting the situation with the bias of "I'm vulnerable, others might hurt me, this is dangerous, and I'm useless and unlovable".

The mind will work to make any contrary information, fit with those beliefs.

This is how a client may present due to their history and how they may now interpret the world. We need to

Introduction to Counselling Skills and Theory

understand their world and help them to experience a safe world by bringing them to awareness of how their past experiences may be impacting on the now.

What do you see?

An old woman or a young girl?

Discovering new perspectives needs to be handled with skill and care in a one to one session.

We need to ensure that the client doesn't feel:

1. The problem is diminished by over-simplification

2. Inadequate for not finding their own solution

Introduction to Counselling Skills and Theory

3. That we are disrespectful of their life situation

4. That we have dismissed their world and views

If you are going to help your client to see things from a new perspective, then consider the following:

- That this is about how you feel

- Acknowledge that the client may find your viewpoint challenging

- Explain that you are taking a risk and that you are investing in the relationship

- Make a direct statement laying out your views clearly

When exploring alternative perspectives with a client I will show them a blank piece of A4 paper with a dot in the middle and ask. What do you see?

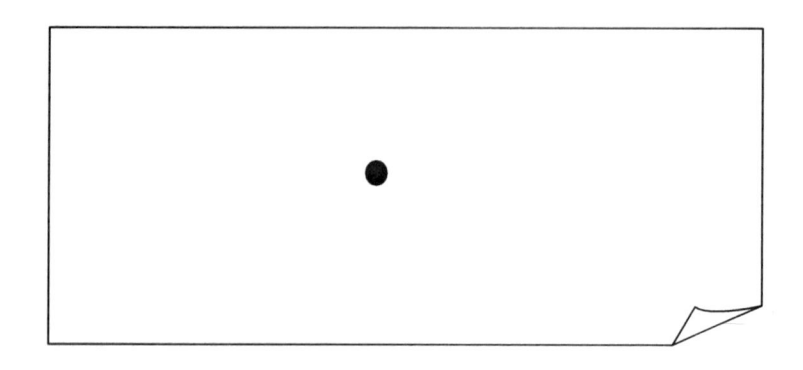

Introduction to Counselling Skills and Theory

The client will usually say "a black dot." I point out to them that it is interesting that they saw the 'black dot' and yet there is a whole sheet of white paper here.

I then use their problem to show them how this relates to their own perspective. So let's say its "My girlfriend must have dumped me as she promised to phone and she didn't."

The dot in the middle is the client's perspective, let's look at some alternatives

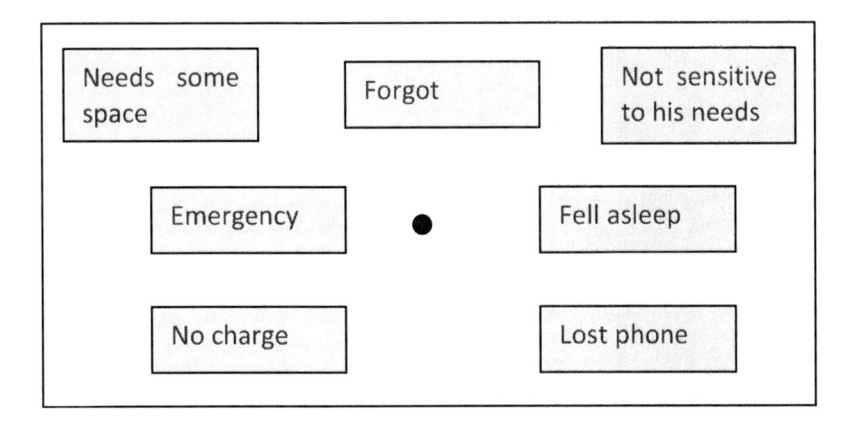

Needs some space	Forgot	Not sensitive to his needs
Emergency	●	Fell asleep
No charge		Lost phone

The client will come up with 'new perspectives' once you get him thinking more logically, and indeed she may have 'dumped him,' but at that point there was no evidence to support this belief and until there is it is not definitely the truth.

As usual when doing this be tentative and sensitive to the client's wellbeing.

Introduction to Counselling Skills and Theory

Thoughts:

How do you see your world?

What perceptions do you have that differ from other significant people in your life?

Introduction to Counselling Skills and Theory

Chapter 19
Challenge

Many trainees struggle with this part of their training. They disclose feeling that they would be uncomfortable with challenging clients. This does not surprise me as it's something we are uncomfortable with in our daily lives.

The word 'challenge' alone is quite threatening, and most of us would run for the hills if we thought that we were going to have to challenge someone or be challenged ourselves.

Try changing the word to "feedback to grow" or "checking this out" because certainly in the counselling sense this is what we are doing.

Challenge is something most therapists do deliberately and consciously as a strategy, so we need to work through our fears of this word or activity.

Introduction to Counselling Skills and Theory

In counselling challenge is a skill which needs to be implemented with great sensitivity. There is a fine line between helpful challenge and destructive challenge. As therapists we most definitely need to learn the art of 'helpful challenge'.

We also need to feel comfortable with being challenged ourselves as if we are not then we will find it difficult to challenge others. Here is a model that helps us to understand the concept of the most helpful way to challenge:

HIGH CHALLENGE

Too scary, we get too frightened, defensive or hostile	The right balance for active participation in self exploration. Exciting stuff!!!!
LOW SUPPORT	**HIGH SUPPORT**
Too dull, we become bored, disinterested and lose heart.	Too comfy and cosy, we don't get much work done.

LOW CHALLENGE

Introduction to Counselling Skills and Theory

From this model you can see that to highly challenge your client where you also offer a high level of support it can be the right balance for active participation from your client and they will participate in self exploration.

The aim of challenge as a skill is to:

- ✓ Look at other viewpoints
- ✓ Accept the value of other viewpoints
- ✓ Look at their own behaviour and its impact on others
- ✓ To explore and change irrational thought processes
- ✓ To explore hidden feelings

To do this sensitively you need to think about:

- ✓ Whether the person you are helping is up for it
- ✓ Being specific not vague
- ✓ Not making it the clients fault or blame them
- ✓ Set a good example by accepting challenges from the person you are trying to help

Introduction to Counselling Skills and Theory

✓ Always be tentative

You need to consider that challenging ineffectively can:

✗ Create a loss of trust

✗ A breakdown in the relationship

However challenge can be an affirmation of the strength of a relationship if done effectively.

Typical areas of challenge (although it is important to emphasize that challenge must always be tentative, gentle but firm and specific).

- Discrepancies and contradictions: "You say you are sad and yet you are smiling" or "You say that you cannot hold your own in an argument and yet you argued with me in our last session"

- Ways of thinking: A particular area for CBT counsellors. To challenge irrational thoughts and beliefs.

- Vagueness or apparent confusion: "You say that you are confused about your parent's behaviour and the impact it has on your own?"

- Making someone or something else responsible for

Introduction to Counselling Skills and Theory

the problem: "I wonder if you could perhaps own some of what is happening to you?" "I'm sensing that you feel that your wife is fully to blame for this, and I wonder if this is completely true?"

If you take the **LLE** out of CHALLENGE then you get:

CHA NGE

THEREFORE

CHALLENGE = CHANGE.

Thoughts:

How comfortable are you with challenge?

Are you able to challenge others in a helpful way?

How do you feel when you are challenged?

Introduction to Counselling Skills and Theory

**Chapter 20
Personal Development
Container**

Creative tools are sometimes used (i.e art, music, stories, poetry, quotes or metaphors) in therapists work with clients. They can often be used with students doing personal development too. The rationale is to help you to explore, express and understand important feelings and thoughts in a safe way.

They can also help you to become aware of feelings that are not currently in your conscious awareness. Sometimes it is difficult to put into words your thoughts and feelings. Creativity can help you to do this. It can invoke fun, inspiration and excitement in the therapeutic journey.

The imagination is a wonderful thing when used in a positive way, and can help you to move forward in heaps and bounds. Try the exercise on the following page.

Introduction to Counselling Skills and Theory

1. Imagine you are a container which container would you be?

2. How useful am I?

3. How do I feel as the container?

4. What do people do with me?

5. How do you see yourself?

6. How do you think others see you?

7. Would you like to change?

8. Where do I belong?

9. Given a free choice what container would you choose to be and why?

Introduction to Counselling Skills and Theory

Now look at your answers:

What are they telling you?

Is there a link between what is going on in your life right now?

Are your answers telling you where you may need to make changes?

If not do not worry not every tool works for everyone and maybe life is running pretty smoothly for you at present.

Introduction to Counselling Skills and Theory

Chapter 21
Egans three stage model & goal setting

Another skill that you will learn in your counselling training is goal setting or sometimes known as action planning. Clients may need to set goals to enable them to change their current situation and of course you will be able to help them in doing this.

The skills that you are learning may now be starting to confuse you and you may be feeling dizzy with all that you need to learn. For that reason I am going to show you **Egan's three stage model** to enable you to feel a little more confident in what you are doing.

Gerard Egan published the first edition of his book **"The skilled helper"** in 1975. He wanted to translate the core conditions into a set of identifiable skills. He added to the ideas of **Carl Rogers** by taking the work of other psychologists and developed a theory of helping based on the skills required at different stages of the helping

Introduction to Counselling Skills and Theory

process. Egan felt that the core conditions are a necessary requirement of the helping relationship however he did not believe that standing alone they were enough. He felt that they needed extra tools before helping would be effective.

Gerard Egan discussed three stages in the helping process and he developed a model to emphasise this. The three stage model.

Stage One
Building the helping relationship and exploration.

Stage Two
New understanding and offering new perspectives

Stage Three
Action - helping the client to develop and use helping strategies

He described the stages as follows:

Stage One – The current scenario – "What is here?"

Introduction to Counselling Skills and Theory

This is about building a trusting relationship with the client and helping them to explore and clarify their problem situation. It deals with what is happening now for the client.

Skills:

The skills that you would use at this stage are:

- ✓ Core conditions
- ✓ Active listening
- ✓ Attending to behaviour and feeling
- ✓ Reflection
- ✓ Paraphrase
- ✓ Summarise
- ✓ Clarify

Stage Two – Preferred scenario – "What do I want here?"

This is about helping the client to identify what they want. It is about identifying what options are open to the client.

Skills:

Introduction to Counselling Skills and Theory

The skills he discussed would be needed here are:

- ✓ Identifying themes
- ✓ Focusing
- ✓ Offering alternative perspectives
- ✓ Sharing therapist experience/feelings (immediacy)

Stage Three – Actions – "How might I help this to happen"

This is about supporting the client to look at how they might help themselves. It is about looking at possible outcomes.

Skills:

The skills needed for this stage are:

- ✓ Facilitate client in developing and choosing ways to help self.
- ✓ Helping client to consider and evaluate choices

Stage three is where we help the client to explore an action plan that will support them in change. Counselling is about 'change'.

Introduction to Counselling Skills and Theory

Goal setting

Goal setting with your client could be anything from deciding to change their job, to behaviour change, cognitive change or coming to terms with their historical experiences, or awareness of how that history is impacting on their present, the unhelpful strategies that they use to cope and finding new strategies.

There are many tools around on the internet to help people to goal set; one that is popular today is **SMART.** This is a tool to help you to set goals that your client will be able to achieve, that are not too farfetched, so that the client is not set up for failure.

Specific - A specific goal has a much greater chance of being accomplished than a general goal. To set a specific goal you must answer the six "W" questions: Who, what, where, when, which and why.

Measurable - When you measure your progress, you stay on track, reach your target dates, and experience the exhilaration of achievement that spurs you on to continued effort required to reach your goal.

Achievable - When you identify goals that are most important to you, you begin to figure out ways you can make them come true.

Introduction to Counselling Skills and Theory

Realistic - To be realistic, a goal must represent an objective toward which you are both *willing* and *able* to work. A goal can be both high and realistic; you are the only one who can decide just how high your goal should be.

Timely - A goal should be grounded within a time frame. With no time frame tied to it there's no sense of urgency. If you want to lose 10 lbs, when do you want to lose it by? "Someday" won't work. But if you anchor it within a timeframe, "by May 1st", then you've set your unconscious mind into motion to begin working on the goal.

Clients may come along and be 'all over the place,' jumping from one thing to another it is sometimes referred to as 'Island hopping' or 'going off on a tangent'. It is very hard when clients are in this frame of mind to set goals. They may be in ambivalence or just feel overloaded with problems.

It is important that you don't rush into this stage and push clients into goal setting.

They may need to process first. Allow them time to process. After all, when we have a problem with the washing machine or dvd player we don't go straight into

Introduction to Counselling Skills and Theory

'fixing it,' we troubleshoot first. This may be the client's way of trouble shooting.

It is important that your clients are given the space to get everything out. Sometimes however, particularly if we are doing short term therapy, they have a lot of problems, and we only have the time to help them with one of those problems, therefore it is important to help clients to focus too.

A useful tool for this if you feel it would be helpful to move your client forward is to say:

"I notice that you have several issues that you are bringing to therapy. I wonder if it would be helpful if we did a problem list to prioritize your problems and explore where you might get the right kind of help"

If the client agrees then you can do this. However in longer term therapy and particularly Person Centered Therapy, you would perhaps stay with this stuckness.

Problem List:

PROBLEM	PRIORITY	RESOURCE
Stress in job	4	Explore in therapy
Putting on weight	7	Weight watchers
Children leaving home	5	Explore in therapy

Introduction to Counselling Skills and Theory

Wife going out a lot	3	Explore with wife
Want to give up smoking	6	Smoking cessation
Rent arrears	2	CAB & Council
No time out/relaxation	1	Explore in therapy

All of those problems would be far too much to cover in time limited sessions. In this current climate many job opportunities for counsellors are for brief interventions, so this list will help you to stay focused as well as the client. This model has enabled the client to prioritise his problems and look at where else he may get support.

His priority in terms of the work he wants to do in therapy is:

- ✓ Relaxation – This may also help with his stress in his job and may help with his feelings re his children leaving home.

Thoughts:

Write out your own problem list and use the SMART model to set some goals for yourself.

Introduction to Counselling Skills and Theory

Chapter 22
Maslow Hierarchy of needs

Maslow's theories run parallel to those of Carl Rogers. He created a model that places motivational needs in a hierarch and suggests that before more sophisticated, higher order needs can be met, certain primary needs must be satisfied.

He demonstrates this on a triangle with the more fundamental, lower order needs at the base and the higher level needs at the top.

This became known as Maslow's Hierarchy of needs.

Maslow's hierarchy of needs is used in many areas of training today. It is particularly used on teachers training courses and management courses, to give learners a better understanding of how to get the most out of their students/workforce.

Maslow's Hierarchy of needs

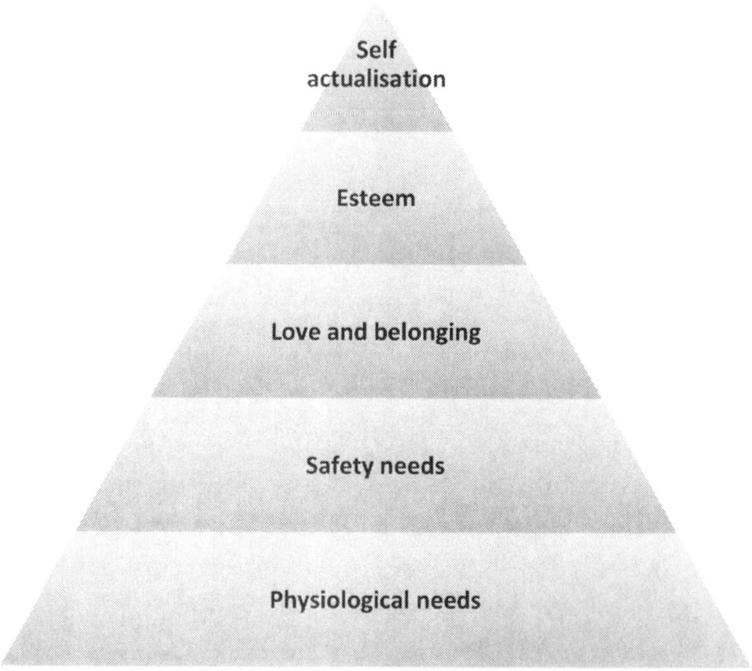
Self actualisation
Esteem
Love and belonging
Safety needs
Physiological needs

Physiological Needs:

Maslow believed that these needs are the most basic and instinctive needs in the hierarchy because all needs become secondary until these physiological needs are met.

Introduction to Counselling Skills and Theory

They include:

- Food
- Sleep
- Air
- Water
- Sex
- Bodily comfort

Safety Needs:

The safety and security is needed after the physical needs have been met. Security needs are important for survival.

They are:

- Health and wellbeing
- Safe neighbourhood
- Financial security
- Job security

Love and belonging:

Introduction to Counselling Skills and Theory

As human beings we have the need to love and to be loved by others.

- Family
- Intimacy
- Friendship

The need to feel a sense of belonging and acceptance by:

- Sports team
- Religious group
- Clubs
- Social groups

Esteem:

Humans have a need to have self esteem and self respect. Esteem presents the normal human desire to be accepted and valued by others.

There are two kinds of self esteem.

High self esteem:

- The need for strength

Introduction to Counselling Skills and Theory

- Competence
- Mastery
- Self confidence
- Independence and freedom

Low self esteem:

- The need for status
- Recognition
- Fame
- Prestige
- Attention

Self actualisation:

This level of need pertains to what a person's full potential is and realising that potential. Maslow describes this desire as the desire to become more and more what one is, to become everything that one is capable of becoming.

Self actualised people are:

Introduction to Counselling Skills and Theory

- Self aware

- Concerned with personal growth

- Less concerned with the opinions of others

- Interested in fulfilling their potential

- They have an accurate perception of reality and can view people in an unbiased way

- They accept themselves and others and recognise their limitations and those of others

- They tend to be spontaneous people

- They are more problem centred

- They are emotionally self sufficient

- They remain un-jaded by life

- They are independent of the world around them

- They have empathy for others

- They have few deep relationships

- They have very definite moral standards

Introduction to Counselling Skills and Theory

- They have a philosophical sense of humour

- They are highly creative

- They appreciate the unexpected, they enjoy surprises

How many of these can you tick off now as being where you are in life. Do this now and then do it again at the end of your training and compare the difference.

Maslow says we all have the potential to reach our full potential.

Where are you in terms of your full potential?

What is your full potential?

What needs do you need to explore before reaching your full potential?

Remember everyone's full potential is different; it is always about the clients full potential.

When a client comes into therapy s/he will have needs. Those needs will be in order of priority, the client's priority, not ours.

For example:

Introduction to Counselling Skills and Theory

A drug using client accessing therapy to address his addiction:

Self actualisation

Self esteem
(He has a low self esteem........)

Love and belongingness
(He has no contact with family or friends.........)

Safety & Security
(He has no home or job...........)

Physiological needs
(He has no food............)

It will be very difficult to work with his psychological needs while he is homeless, hungry and lonely.

So these needs may need attending to before the psychological work is done. If you attempt the psychological work first then it is unlikely to be effective.

For example:

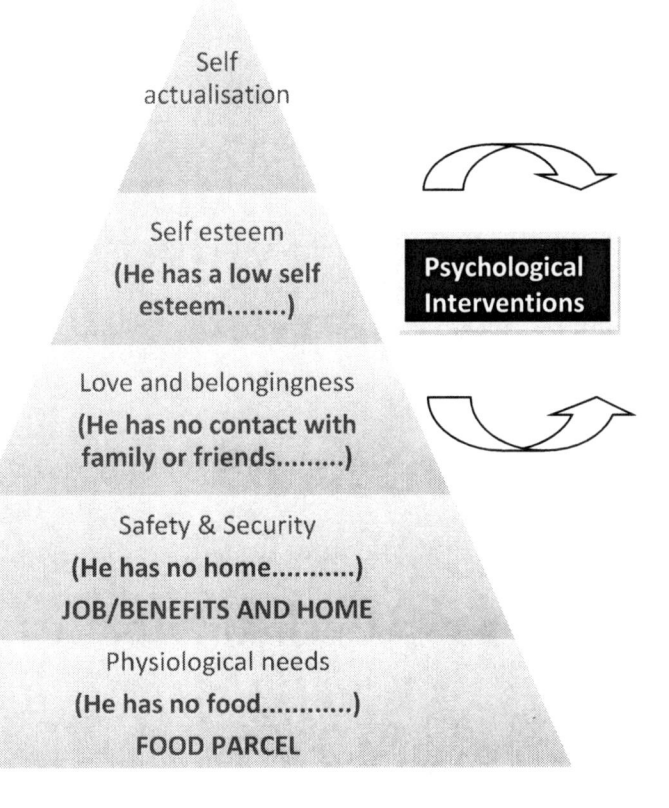

Introduction to Counselling Skills and Theory

```
                    Self
                 actualisation

                  Self esteem
               (He has a low self      Psychological
                  esteem........)      Interventions

              Love and belongingness
              (He has no contact with
                family or friends.........)

              Safety & Security
              (He has no home............)
              JOB/BENEFITS AND HOME

             Physiological needs
             (He has no food............)
             FOOD PARCEL
```

This is when psychological interventions may be appropriate, once the clients more basic needs are met.

Those interventions may be:

- Improvement in relationships

- Improve self esteem

Introduction to Counselling Skills and Theory

- Encourage self growth

If you try to work with something in a different order to the client's needs then s/he will just block the progress.

In terms of my example, if I had tried to work with the clients self esteem whilst s/he was starving and homeless it would be doubtful that I would get anywhere.

Maslow's Hierarchy of needs is used in the counselling training to:

- Support you in understanding how and when a client comes into the therapy room, and the varied places that they might be in, in their lives.

- Understand a client's ambivalence.

- Help you to understand that there are certain needs that may require being met before any psychological work can be done.

- See things from a systemic viewpoint.

- See that there might be a need for referral, support or co working with other agencies.

- Support the client in getting basic needs met before psychological work begins.

Introduction to Counselling Skills and Theory

A lot of counselling courses will teach you about **Maslow's** hierarchy of needs.

Thoughts:

Does person centred therapy..........

- Give the client permission to only bring safe material and hold back on more painful/dangerous subjects, protecting themselves from deep emotional disturbance?

- Does resistance need to be challenged by the therapist in order to make progress/reach self actualisation?
OR
- Does offering the core conditions alone minimise the clients resistance?

Introduction to Counselling Skills and Theory

Chapter Twenty Three
Your own personal style, reflective practice & competency model

When learning new counselling skills the task is to combine the technical ability to do the skill with our own unique way of performing it. We are all unique and very different in our ways of communicating. I have seen some very different counsellors in my time, very good but very unique in their style.

We can learn all these new skills and work very hard at using them and in the midst of this loose an important part of our personality, the part of us that we are loved and admired for. I remember in my own training becoming so 'adult' and 'professional' that one of my closest friends said where is the Linda that I used to have fun with, the creative Linda?

We can still take that part of us into the therapy room; we can still have fun and be creative.

Introduction to Counselling Skills and Theory

Our personal style is what makes the skills in counselling come to life. When giving feedback it is important to recognise and feedback on a helpers style.

The most significant skill that you can develop as a therapist is 'self reflection'. We have done a lot of this in this book, both at the end of the chapters and in the personal development chapters. But, it just doesn't stop there.

We must 'reflect on our practice' too. The second most important skill after seeing the client is to learn to reflect on the session you had with the client. It is almost like having an internal supervisor.

- ✓ What worked?
- ✓ What didn't work?
- ✓ What theoretical approach did I use with this client?
- ✓ What is the clients learning style? (Does he respond better to metaphor, pictures, diagrams etc)
- ✓ What are your strengths?
- ✓ What are your weaknesses?

Introduction to Counselling Skills and Theory

- ✓ Did the client fail to attend, if so why might that be?

- ✓ What is the therapeutic relationship like?

- ✓ How was I feeling and what made me feel that way?

- ✓ What was I trying to achieve?

- ✓ How might I respond differently if this situation was to arise again?

- ✓ What issues seemed significant enough to pay attention to?

- ✓ What was the client not saying?

- ✓ How does this client relate to me?

- ✓ How do I feel NOW about this experience?

- ✓ What may I need to take to clinical supervision to explore?

- ✓ Am I using the appropriate frameworks?

- ✓ Am I working safely?

- ✓ Have I any prejudices towards this client?

Introduction to Counselling Skills and Theory

✓ What irritates me about this client?

And so on, and so on.

Self reflection is a way of evaluating our own role within the relationship. Taking our own beliefs, values and bias's into account. It assists the therapist to be aware where their motives and actions stem from in order to make them a more effective practitioner in dealing with unique people in unique scenarios. This is what you will already be doing in your skills practice and your journal is where you will write about this.

Competency Matrix

Training to be a counsellor can be very frustrating, there will be many times when you will feel deskilled or I am not cut out for this. This is normal.

This is all part of your growth. Any counsellor in training that did not go through this would be concerning. We have to go through the muddle to learn. You are learning a whole new set of skills, a whole new way of being. It is a little like learning to drive a car. At first you are unconsciously incompetent, concentrating on the gears, the break, the mirrors, the steering wheel. Then one day you drive from A to B and can't remember the bit in the middle. Counselling training is similar. See competency matrix on next page.

Introduction to Counselling Skills and Theory

COMPETENCY MATRIX

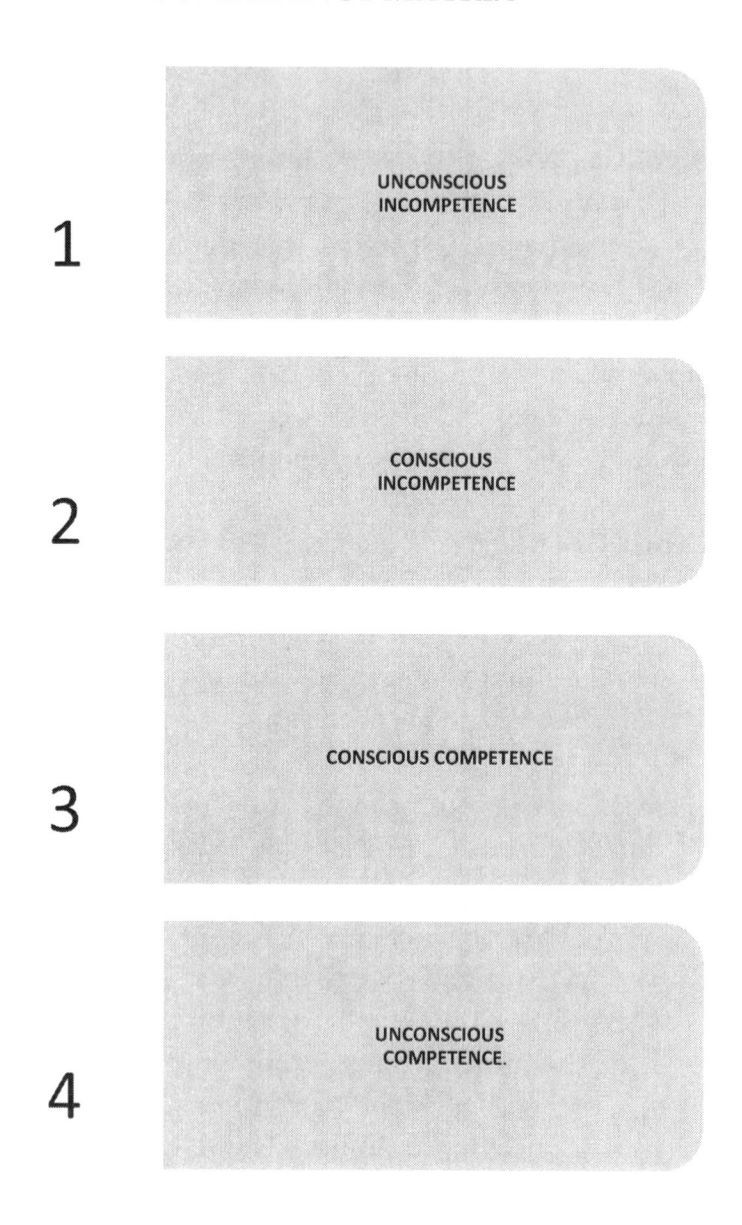

1. UNCONSCIOUS INCOMPETENCE

2. CONSCIOUS INCOMPETENCE

3. CONSCIOUS COMPETENCE

4. UNCONSCIOUS COMPETENCE.

Introduction to Counselling Skills and Theory

Which means:

UNCONSCIOUS INCOMPETENCE

We don't know what skills are needed, nor do we know what skills we have or don't have after practice. We move on to............

CONSCIOUS INCOMPETENCE

When we start recognising skills that we need, but don't have. This is the frustrating and sometimes soul destroying phase. Next comes........

CONSCIOUS COMPETENCE

When we have to concentrate like crazy in order to keep the skill going and it feels really awkward and artificial. Finally we arrive at ....

UNCONSCIOUS COMPETENCE

When we can take our hands off the handlebars and whistle as we go along. The activity that once felt variously impossible, or just possible but awkward and wooden now becomes second nature.

Therefore, all that you may go through is quite normal when learning a new skill.

Introduction to Counselling Skills and Theory

Thoughts:

Make a list of the counselling skills you have been shown so far and against each one note where in the cycle you are.

- ✓ Unconscious incompetence
- ✓ Conscious incompetence
- ✓ Conscious competence
- ✓ Unconscious competence

Introduction to Counselling Skills and Theory

Chapter 24
Taped assignment and Case study and critical evaluations

As part of the assessment criteria you may be asked to do a taped (either CD or DVD) assignment and a critical evaluation of your practice.

The purpose of video assessment is:

- ✓ To assess the extent to which appropriate counselling/intervention skills, strategies, techniques and methods are being used on a specific occasion.
- ✓ To assess the appropriateness of the intervention,
- ✓ To assess the extent to which you are a safe practitioner.

Remember that the recording should be illustrating your input to the session, how you obtained the necessary

Introduction to Counselling Skills and Theory

information and demonstrate how you generally treated the client.

The entire session must be recorded. Ensure that there is an introduction, a core of intervention and a termination to the session, all in the time allotted.

The framing of the therapist should be more than just head and shoulders. The shot should be from the waist to just above the head. The therapist and the setting will occupy roughly equal areas in the frame and there should be space for the therapist's hand gestures to be seen.

The critical evaluation should explore the key moments in the session and relate the content of the session to relevant theory and practice guidelines. It needs to explain why you carried out particular tasks in the session or responded in the way you did to the client's statements or behaviour.

It should also discuss the quality of the intervention shown on the video and highlight any ways in which the intervention could be improved or modified as appropriate. It should describe the literature which you used to support your work.

Watch your video recording as much as you need to in writing up your essay. The critical evaluation is as it says an evaluation of your work and should be more analytical

Introduction to Counselling Skills and Theory

than descriptive (we can see what you have done from the recording).

You need to demonstrate the sense you made of the information or responses gained, the conclusion you reached about the severity of the problems, the intervention you offered and any further intervention plans you have made.

There must be an introduction with sufficient background information for the context of the session to be intelligible, and to include the age, gender of your client, the presenting problem and how s/he presented. The introduction need be no more than one hundred words.

The introduction should then be followed by a comprehensive written analysis of the content of the assignment.

You should be willing to address the positive and less positive aspects of your practice evident in the recording. If you feel you could have dealt with an aspect in a more constructive manner, the alternative style or approach should be mentioned in the essay.

Any references to support your practice should be recorded in line with the guidelines for referencing for written assignments.

Introduction to Counselling Skills and Theory

The following aspects must then be addressed as separate sections.

- ✓ Describe the aim of the session including how the structure of the session was planned.

- ✓ A discussion of the key moments of what you said and did and how you demonstrated that you were pursuing the plan.

- ✓ A discussion of the extent to which you achieved what you set out to achieve

In each section you need to give an adequate flavour of the skills you were using, without resorting to analysing every single sentence. Simply identify these skills and comment on why you thought they were appropriate. Throughout the report you should refer to relevant theory and research.

Example:

> My client is female and aged 35. She presented in an agitated way, looking quite nervous about the therapy. Her presenting problems was the breakdown of her relationship after fifteen years, which has left her perplexed and lost as she found herself directed and told what to do by her husband and now that he is out of the equation she is finding it hard to know what to do and more importantly who she really is.

Introduction to Counselling Skills and Theory

This tape is our first session together, and I started by welcoming her to the session by stating that everything we discussed would remain in the room and between us (confidentiality) and that we had 20 minutes in which to explore any concerns she may have. I told her that the session would be taped and why. I did this in a warm empathic way to facilitate an understanding relationship and to hopefully settle her nerves about therapy, and about being taped.

During the session I helped the client to explore some concerns in regards to a long term relationship that came to a sudden end. I allowed her the space to explore how this has impacted on her sense of direction in life using active listening skills, silence and para verbals.

I paraphrased her feelings regarding not knowing who she is, since the absence of her partner. I feel that I helped the client through my interventions to explore her sense of 'self' now that she has found herself on her own. She disclosed how she left college without finishing her studies after finding herself pregnant at a young age. She was able to discuss a desire to go back to college and revisit her studies now that her children are more independent.

I felt that I was being empathic towards the client, in the understanding of what she had said to me.

Introduction to Counselling Skills and Theory

Empathic understanding is described as *"being able to stand back far enough to remain objective, rather than standing too close and risk becoming enmeshed in the client's world"* **(Sutton and Stewart, 2008, pg 35)**

I saw myself as being empathic through trying to see what the client had said to me through her frame of reference and not mine.

The client asked me if I thought she was stupid in being so dependent on her ex partner. I responded with "I am more interested in what you think about yourself" which I felt was a non judgemental response to the client, which is another of Roger's therapeutic conditions.

My client then went on to say "I should have been less reliant on my partner. I was so needy." I feel that I wish I would have picked up on that and asked her to clarify what she meant, especially now looking back on the tape and noticed that she said this or similar a few times during our session. The client may have felt that she was ignored, or worse I was agreeing with her by my lack of acknowledgement.

Later in the tape she talked about her role within the marriage and how she did all the domestic duties, sorted all the bills out and the children's activities. I could have linked this to her earlier statement and used sensitive challenge by saying something like "It sounds as if you were quite independent in the relationship. However you

Introduction to Counselling Skills and Theory

said earlier that you were reliant on your partner and needy?" This may have empowered her to see how capable she is.

This was possibly lack of congruence on my part as I believe in hindsight that I could have brought this to the attention of the client.

Congruence (the third of Rogers' therapeutic conditions) is *"the state of being of the counsellor when her outward responses to her client consistently match her inner experiencing of her client"*. **(Mearns and Thorne, 2008, pg 121)**

Most of my interventions were reflecting content back to her or paraphrasing, just to help her explore what she said to me and establish a mutual understanding of what was being said. Paraphrasing is: " **reflecting back the client's communication in your own words, bringing clarification**" **(Sutton and Stewart, 2008, pg 95)**

I feel I was being as attentive a listener as I could have been, although as I said above there were a couple of incidents where I missed out on reflecting back to the speaker what I had heard and I put this down as possible lack of congruence at that time. Although in hindsight I recognise that 'challenge' is a skill that I need to work on to improve my practice. I need to recognise that it is incongruent of me to ignore my client's inconsistencies and I missed an opportunity to reflect this back.

Introduction to Counselling Skills and Theory

I feel that before I started the course, I would have given this client advice and told her that she may be better off without her husband, so I recognise that my skills are very different now and that I am more empathic towards people's problems. For me to progress I should try to explore my feelings more, rather than holding back at times, as this can cause problems or restrictions in regards to my skills work. This was highlighted by the way I felt in the tape, and I think this limits my congruence towards the situation and the speaker, which may prevent crucial points being explored.

As far as the other two core conditions go: empathy and U.P.R, I feel that I express them as far as my capabilities as a provider of counselling skills goes, although I do see myself relying on reflection and paraphrasing a lot but I still feel that my reflective responses carry within them levels of U.P.R and empathy. I feel that I can achieve the absences in my skills work through greater openness and to use my personal learning journal more effectively.

It is important in this assignment to talk about your weaknesses just as much as your strengths. If this assignment spoke only about 'how good you were', then be mindful that this would be a fail or be referred.

Good Luck.

Introduction to Counselling Skills and Theory

Chapter 25
Personal Development
Developing a more nurturing self

As trainee counsellors and indeed practicing counsellors we need to develop a more nurturing self. As human beings we seem to be very good at nurturing others but not so well at nurturing ourselves. Building a loving and caring relationship with yourself enables you to develop a loving and caring relationship with others. It helps in the following ways:

- ✓ To nurture a good self esteem
- ✓ To relieve stress
- ✓ To encourage healthy thoughts, feelings and behaviour
- ✓ To support physical health

Have a go at the exercise on the following page and explore ways, in which you might nurture yourself.

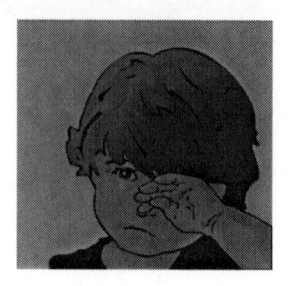

Introduction to Counselling Skills and Theory

If a child was in pain, what would you do?

1..

2..

3..

4..

5..

6..

7..

8..

9..

10..

These strategies can be ones you use to nurture yourself.

Introduction to Counselling Skills and Theory

Chapter 26
Confidentiality & Framework for ethical practice

When working with clients it is important that the terms and conditions of the counselling process are established as soon as possible in order to avoid confusion and possible complaints about breaches of confidentiality.

In a lot of services during the first call counsellors are asked to establish the ground rules and demonstrate that they have been communicated by use of tick boxes. (Service entitlement/confidentiality etc).

If these issues are not discussed it is vital that this is indicated by omitting the tick in the appropriate box and noting in the body of the notes/supervision why this has not been done. (It is appreciated that some calls are very short or info only and clearly it is inappropriate to begin to go into details involving client confidentiality during these contacts).

Introduction to Counselling Skills and Theory

A client's entitlement to confidentiality is legally enforceable at common law and the client can sue for breach of an expressed or implied contractual term.

Counsellors are expected to be as conscientious in maintaining confidentiality as a priest or doctor. Nonetheless, this duty is not absolute. Only barristers and solicitors have a theoretical absolute legal privilege of not having to disclose information given to them by clients.

The law does recognise that counsellors may choose to breach confidentiality under certain circumstances. The responsibility for this breach rests with the counsellor, who would be responsible/accountable for that decision.

In most services if a counsellor or professional feels that s/he needs to break a person's confidence then they will have a policy in place. This may be to contact their line manager or clinical supervisor.

A breach of confidentiality is defensible in the following circumstances:

- The client has consented to disclosure

- The confidences disclosed are already public knowledge

- The balance between the public interest in the maintenance of confidentiality is outweighed by

Introduction to Counselling Skills and Theory

the public interest in disclosure. (This last circumstance is sometimes applicable where a 'safety critical' scheme is involved/innocent people are at significant risk)

- The counsellor has good evidence to support a claim that 'the client was no longer willing or able to take responsibility for his/her actions.' (BACP B.3.4. 1)

Counsellors need to be aware that:

The BACP Code of Ethics B.3.2.states that 'the counselling contract will include an agreement about the level and limits of confidentiality offered'.

'Counsellors must ensure that they have taken all reasonable steps to inform the client of any limitations to confidentiality that arise within the setting of the counselling work' (B.3.3.1) e.g. use of internal supervision.'

When a counsellor is considering a breach of confidentiality they must be aware that the client needs to be informed that the counsellor intends to discuss this with his/her supervisor/Manager or other agencies.

'Informed by Counselling, Confidentiality and the Law. BACP Information Guide 1. 1994

Introduction to Counselling Skills and Theory

In the event of a Red Flag the counsellor should always inform the client of their intention to breach confidentiality and the possible consequences of such a disclosure (the client can be informed that if they give identifying information they are tacitly agreeing to the counsellor breaching confidentiality)

Please be aware of the BACP'S Code B.3.4.1

Exceptional circumstances may arise which give the counsellor good grounds for believing that serious harm may occur to the client or to other people. In such circumstances the client's consent to a change in the agreement about confidentiality should be sought whenever possible unless there are also good grounds for believing the client is no longer willing or able to take responsibility for his/her actions.

Normally, the decision to break confidentiality should be discussed with the client and should be made only after consultation with the counselling supervisor or if he/she is not available an experienced counsellor.

My confidentiality contract to my clients was:

"Everything you tell me is confidential unless you tell me that you are **going** to harm yourself or others, commit a terrorist act or an act against children"

There was a major flaw in this why?

Introduction to Counselling Skills and Theory

What if someone told you of a serious crime they planned on committing i.e armed robbery or a serious unresolved crime that they had committed in the past.

We have a right to break a clients confidentiality when they disclose:

- ✓ Risk to self or others
- ✓ Child protection issues
- ✓ Plan to commit a serious crime (including an act of terrorism)
- ✓ Or a serious unresolved crime from the past

If you are working within an organisation and discuss clients in clinical team meetings, then it is perhaps being congruent if you tell the client that 'it is confidential to the service.'

You may also want to tell your client that you sometimes may need to discuss him or her in clinical supervision. However may not use their name (if this is true of course).

The British association of counselling and psychotherapy ethical framework for good practice

Introduction to Counselling Skills and Theory

The British association for counsellors and psychotherapy have developed an ethical framework in which they expect counsellors to work by. These are as follows:

Values:

Respecting human rights and dignity

Protecting the safety of clients

Ensuring the integrity of practitioner-client relationships

Enhancing the quality of professional knowledge and its application

Alleviating personal distress and suffering

Fostering a sense of self that is meaningful to the person(s) concerned

Increasing personal effectiveness

Enhancing the quality of relationships between people

Appreciating the variety of human experience and culture

Striving for the fair and adequate provision of counselling and psychotherapy services

Principals:

Introduction to Counselling Skills and Theory

Being **trustworthy** (honouring the trust placed in the practitioner sometimes known as fidelity)

Autonomy (Respect for the client's right to be self governing)

Beneficence (A commitment to promoting the client's well being)

Non-Maleficence (A commitment to avoiding harm to the client)

Justice (The fair and impartial treatment of all client's and the provision of adequate services)

Self respect (Fostering the practitioners self knowledge and care for self)

Moral qualities:

- Empathy

- Sincerity

- Integrity

- Resilience

Introduction to Counselling Skills and Theory

- Respect

- Humility

- Competence

- Fairness

- Wisdom

- Courage

Thoughts:

Think about confidentiality and the BACP ethical framework for good practice and explore what this means to you.

Why do we need an ethical framework?

Introduction to Counselling Skills and Theory

Chapter 27
Supervision & working safely

This chapter covers the different forms of workplace supervision, and counselling supervision and the importance of clinical supervision when practising as a counsellor.

Managerial supervision is someone who is responsible for things such as:

- Induction
- Appraisals
- Holidays/sick leave/time off
- Disciplinary issues
- Lateness

Introduction to Counselling Skills and Theory

- Workload

Clinical supervision is the person who is responsible for the supervision of your cases – the work that you do with clients.

- Ethical issues

- Confidential issues

- Caseload issues

- Feeling Stuck in client work

- Relationships with counsellors

- Reflection on practice

- Treatment plan

- Transference issues

- Risk issues

The purpose of clinical supervision as well as supporting you with the above is to assist the practitioner to learn from his or her experience and progress in expertise, as well as to ensure good service to the client or patient.

Introduction to Counselling Skills and Theory

The current BACP guidelines are one hour for every eight hours of client work for an experienced counsellor. However, if working with more complex clients then the therapist may need more.

The clinical supervisor acts not as a 'boss', but as a consultant.

Supervision exists for two reasons:

1. To protect clients and

2. To improve the ability of counsellors to provide value to their clients.

Supervision protects clients by involving an impartial third party in the work of a counsellor and client, helping to reduce risk of serious oversight and helping the counsellor to reflect on their own feelings, thoughts and behaviour and general approach with the client.

All practising counsellors and psychotherapists **must** have clinical supervision. To work without supervision is working unsafely. To go without counselling supervision puts you at risk of losing your licence to practice and leaves you open to being sued for malpractice.

Working safely.

To work safely you need to be mindful of the following:

Introduction to Counselling Skills and Theory

Confidence in your competence.

- We cannot all be an expert in all clients but we need to have confidence in what we do.

- Supervision, continued professional development and feedback will enable us to remain confident in our competence

Confidence in your physical safety

- Make sure that you are familiar with your workplace safety guidelines

- What plans are in place for working with violent clients?

- What are the protocols for clients who are abusive?

- Have you an action plan in place?

Confident that you are supported and backed up

- Support, supervision, training and back up for illness etc.

- Protocols in place for issues such as data protection and confidentiality

Have the Knowledge in terms of:

Introduction to Counselling Skills and Theory

- Familiar with accident reporting etc

- Referrals and additional support for clients

- Familiar with organisational paperwork

<u>Ensuring that you are working within your own limitations</u>

- Your personal limits

- Your professional limits

- The limits of your expertise/experience

- And knowing when to make an appropriate referral

BE AWARE THAT ALTHOUGH WE COVER THIS IN COUNSELLING TRAINING IT IS VERY UNUSUAL FOR A CLIENT TO BE AGGRESSIVE TOWARDS YOU.

However we must cover this topic as we don't want to under emphasize the risk of violence.

- To be on the safe side it is important not to have any sharp or heavy objects in your therapy room as clients can act out their anger, likewise no hot coffee.

Introduction to Counselling Skills and Theory

If someone threatens violence or behaves aggressively without actually hitting out:

- Keep calm

- If you can empathise with them you may

- Realise why they feel so upset

- Get a better idea of how real the threat is

- Be able to let them feel heard

- Remain non judgemental and congruent about their behaviour.

- Never act out your anger.

If someone starts hitting out at the walls, furniture, you or someone else or starts brandishing a weapon the following guidelines might be helpful:

- Stay as calm as you can but remain alert

- Reason with someone only if they stop being violent

- If possible get out and raise the alarm

- Do not intervene if others are fighting

Introduction to Counselling Skills and Theory

- When the incident is over get support or debriefing

- As soon as possible write down what happened in the event the police are involved

If you know a client is violent and has a history of violence particularly towards professionals, take precautions:

- Wear an alarm or sit near a alarm

- Sit close to the door

- Let others know that you are going in with this person

- Leave door slightly ajar

- In severe cases take someone in with you, some client's need to be seen with two people.

As I said earlier it is very rare that a client is violent towards you. I have worked for fifteen years and some of those years with clients who were known to have violent histories and there has never been an incident. Most clients are grateful to be helped.

Clients may sometimes act out their anger in the therapy room, but not usually at you. If I know that I am working

Introduction to Counselling Skills and Theory

with a client with 'anger' issues, then during our initial consultations I will discuss what action we may take if the client gets angry with me. We then make a plan which is usually around 'time out', and returning when things feel cooler for the client.

> **Thoughts:**
>
> Explore your awareness of your own personal safety.
>
> Explore what you might take to supervision if you were working with a client.

Introduction to Counselling Skills and Theory

**Chapter 28
Research assignment**

You may be asked to do a research assignment in your training. This is usually at certificate or diploma level. Your tutor will advise you on the topic and topics vary and could include:

- A counselling organisation (such as Cruise the bereavement service)

- A counselling model (such as Gestalt Therapy)

- A part of a model (such as Jung's personality types or Freud's stages of development – you may be asked to compare two models of the above)

- A counselling issue (such as Grief & Loss or working with addiction)

Introduction to Counselling Skills and Theory

- Occasionally, you may be asked to cover an issue (such as post traumatic stress disorder)

Whatever, the topic a research assignment is what it says and you will be expected to do a lot of research on your topic.

I suggest that you collate the material first. Make lots of notes. Then decide a beginning, middle and end to your assignment.

- The beginning will usually start with the title of your assignment and what you plan to do.

- The middle will be your research and what you have learned through your research, using quotes from the sources that you have read up on.

- The end will be your conclusion.

I use a spider and its legs to help me to do the middle part of the assignment. I would then decide how I was going to start and then read through my research and do a conclusion. I start with the middle because often when doing an assignment most of us 'do not know where to start'; and this can block us from starting.

Try it, it works for me. So, let's say that I am asked to do an assignment on the difference between Person Centred Counselling and Cognitive Behavioural Therapy.

Introduction to Counselling Skills and Theory

I would draw out the following.

Spider Diagram

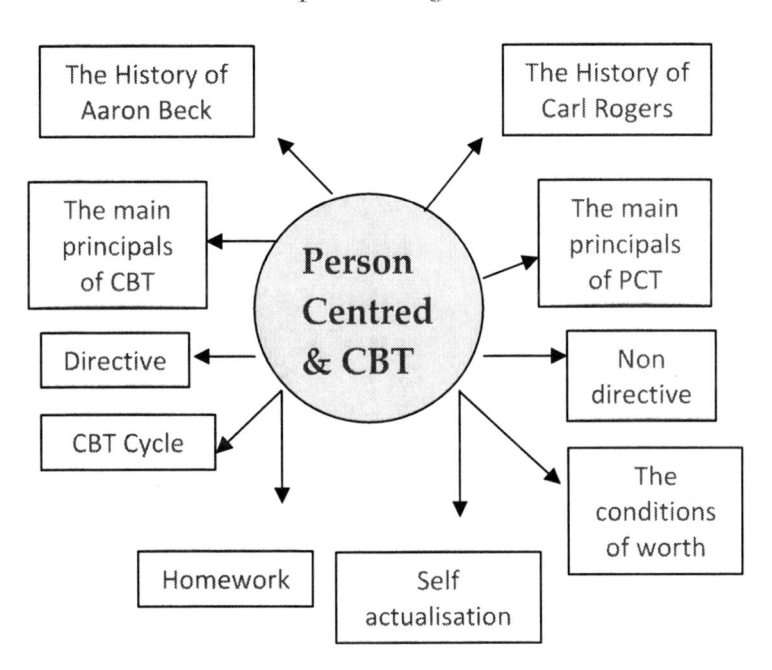

- The History of Aaron Beck
- The History of Carl Rogers
- The main principals of CBT
- The main principals of PCT
- Directive
- Non directive
- CBT Cycle
- The conditions of worth
- Homework
- Self actualisation

(Central topic: **Person Centred & CBT**)

Give yourself plenty of time to do this and read the question thoroughly. Be mindful of presentation and use your spell and grammar check on the computer.

You will possibly be asked to reference your work and do a bibliography. Below is a little about the Harvard referencing guide which will help you to present your work professionally.

Harvard Referencing Quick Guide

Introduction to Counselling Skills and Theory

What is referencing?

Referencing is a system used in the academic community to indicate where ideas, theories, quotes, facts and any other evidence and information used to undertake an assignment, can be found.

Why do I need to reference my work?

⊚ To avoid plagiarism, a form of academic theft.

⊚ Referencing your work correctly ensures that you give appropriate credit to the sources and authors that you have used to complete your assignment.

⊚ Referencing the sources that you have used for your assignment demonstrates that you have undertaken wide-ranging research in order to create your work.

⊚ Referencing your work enables the reader to consult for themselves the same materials that you used.

What do I need to reference?

All the information that you have used in your assignment will need to be acknowledged. It is essential to make a note of all the details of the sources that you use for your assignment as you go along

The basics

Introduction to Counselling Skills and Theory

Harvard is known as the Author & Date system:

1. Citations in the text of your assignment should be made following the in-text guidelines given in the examples on the following pages.

2. A complete list of all the citations used in your text will need to be provided at the end of your assignment. This is called your reference list or bibliography and needs to be presented in alphabetical author/originator order.

Capitals:

Harvard is not prescriptive about capitalisation of authors' names in your reference list. If you do wish to use capitals, then the family/surname of authors are only capitalised in this reference list and **not** in the body of your work. If you prefer not to use capitals in this list, that is fine, but you must be consistent in the style you decide to use.

Italics & underlining:

Only the title of the source of information is italicised or underlined, but you should choose only one method throughout your assignment and stick to it! Do not use both italics and underlining.

Punctuation:

Introduction to Counselling Skills and Theory

Harvard has no one true style of punctuation so the generally accepted rule is to be consistent with your style of punctuation throughout the whole of your assignment.

Introduction to Counselling Skills and Theory

Chapter 29
Transference and Counter transference

Transference is an important part of your learning and is covered more in-depth at Diploma level, however some courses do introduce it at certificate level.

Transference means "to bring past experiences into the present.' Eric Berne simplified this by using the term 'rubber-banding back into a past experience,' or 'putting a face on someone'.

For the most part of this chapter, we will be looking at 'negative transference,' later we will take a look at 'positive transference.'

A simple explanation of 'negative transference,' for those of you who have had children, you may recall spending quite some time thinking about names for the new arrival.

Introduction to Counselling Skills and Theory

Someone may suggest a name of someone you knew from the past. This person may have behaved badly, dressed scruffily, smelt, and had a permanent runny nose or some other characteristic that you did not like. You then discount that name with *"oh no I don't want my child called that"*

A reality check would tell you that this does not mean your baby will be anything like the person in your past; however we rarely do a reality check and often just dismiss the name completely.

This is also sometimes what we do to people, discount them because consciously or unconsciously they remind us of someone we disliked, or treated us badly from our past. This could be 'in' or 'out' of our conscious awareness.

Imagine then if a client came into the room and you took an instant dislike to him or her, without exploring what this might be. Would you be able to build a warm rapport with this client and how might s/he feel.

Some transference is in our awareness, we may say things like *"He's a Gemini, the last Gemini I knew................"*

This could stop you from forming a relationship with a Gemini. Logic tells us that not all Gemini's are the same, and the other Gemini's behaviour is more likely to be

Introduction to Counselling Skills and Theory

down to his/her own experiences, rather than their birth sign.

There are lots of characteristics/behaviours that can trigger conscious transference i.e.

- Eyebrows that meet in the middle
- Someone who drinks heavily
- Someone who sulks
- Clothes/style
- Perfume

Transference that is on a conscious level we can easily reality test if we choose to. We can change our thoughts to "well actually he did not behave in that way just because his eyebrows met in the middle," or other people may reality test our beliefs for us.

However, on an unconscious level, we may take an instant dislike to someone, without knowing why. This may prevent us from developing a relationship with them. We find ourselves saying something like *"I don't know why I don't like her, there's just something about her"*

We may not even recognize what we are doing, just notice feeling uncomfortable around someone, or struggling to

Introduction to Counselling Skills and Theory

relate to a person, or become irritated with a person for no reason at all. We may start to avoid that person due to those feelings and never know why.

These triggers are a lot more subtle, i.e.

- The way someone stands/walks

- The colour/shape of their eyes

- Their colour, shape or gender

- The way they speak/mannerisms

Remember that this is often all out of our own awareness.

To enable you to think about your own transference is there someone in your life that you have avoided, taken an instant dislike to or someone that you are currently in conflict with. Is it your transference? Ask yourself the following questions:

Who do they remind you of from your past?

This may take some time because you are delving deep into your unconscious, if you can't think of anyone carry on reading but come back to those thoughts when you are pottering along in your daily routine.

Introduction to Counselling Skills and Theory

If however you recognise a dislike of this person because they remind you of someone from your past. This is your transference. Ask yourself:

What is it about them that remind you of this person?

Is this evidence enough for you to dislike this person?

This will enable you to work through your transference and separate the past from the present.

How many people have passed through our lives due to our transference? How many relationships with people have we missed out on? Negative transference can block us from forming healthy relationships with others.

If when doing these exercises you found that the person you disliked, avoided or had conflict with did not remind you of anyone from your past, it may not be transference.

Try asking yourself these questions:

Is my attitude towards this person inherited from my parents?

Sometimes we inherit our parent's beliefs about a type of person. For example if your parents gave you messages like 'never trust a man who's eyebrows meet in the middle,' then it's possible that we have inherited the same belief.

Introduction to Counselling Skills and Theory

Reality test that belief.

As adults we do not have to hold on to the beliefs of others. After all think about some of the messages our parents gave us when we were little:

- Eat all your vegetables or you won't have curly hair

- Don't sit on a cold step or you will get piles

- Eat your greens or you will lose your eye sight, you don't see rabbits going into an optician

- Put your tooth under the pillow or the tooth fairy won't come

Do we cling on desperately to those beliefs when we reach adulthood? No we reality test them and discard them. Therefore we can do that with any beliefs that were inherited.

Again if the above is not the case, try this:

Is this person similar to me?

Sometimes others may display characteristics or behaviours similar to our own. These may be the parts of us that we don't like.

Introduction to Counselling Skills and Theory

For example, we may hide the 'weak' side of our self. Therefore we may not like other people who appear weak. Or if part of our personality may be to be opinionated it is highly unlikely that we will relate to another opinionated person.

To further explore this ask yourself:

What do I see in this person that I don't like about myself?

Or it may just be that you don't like this person's behaviour, and it is not transference at all. However the exploration will enable you to see if you are meeting this person 'freely,' developing healthier relationships along the way.

It is extremely important to be able to explore your transference when you are working within the caring profession or working with people in general. That way all the people that you work with will get the same treatment. You will be offering them an empathic, non judgmental and congruent relationship.

In your personal growth it is very important to own your own feelings, and explore them to prevent you from making a hash out of interpersonal relationships, which we can all do at times.

As a therapist it is even more important to explore our transference issues.

Introduction to Counselling Skills and Theory

As well as us having transference towards others be mindful that clients will have transference towards us too, this may affect their ability to form a trusting relationship with us.

We can often internalise other people's dislike for us. We can let it affect us sometimes profoundly, yet it could be down to their transference. It may have nothing to do with us personally.

It is important that we do not internalize their dislike when working in the counseling profession and take our clients 'not liking us' too personally.

If you have a sense that your client is struggling to relate to you or wants to see another therapist accept that it may be their transference and not personal to you.

This learning is to enable you to not take peoples dislike of you personally, and to see that it could be other people's transference. It is for your growth.

We cannot be responsible for other people's transference. We can empathise with their past experience if we know what it is. But, we have no control over it, no matter how much we try to be liked. We can only explore and work on our own transference issues.

Introduction to Counselling Skills and Theory

The idea is to meet people freely, without rubber banding back to the past and without letting your relationships of the present impact on relationships with others.

If relationships are stuck, in conflict, or suffocating, then you now have another tool to explore the process, if you wish.

As well as negative transference, we can also have what is known as positive transference.
This is rubber banding back to positive experiences of people in our past. 'Liking' people because they remind you of someone you liked or whom were good to you in the past. Again, this can be on a conscious level or an unconscious level.

We may, or others may develop a dependency due to this transference. They could see us or we could see others as 'the good mummy' or 'the supportive big sister.'

Be aware that this in itself can create unhealthy relationships and certainly create an unhealthy therapeutic relationship, particularly if you respond with your counter transference.

As well as transference Freud talked about 'counter-transference.' This is <u>our response to someone else's transference.</u>

Introduction to Counselling Skills and Theory

Imagine that you reminded someone of a bully from their schooldays, who had made their lives a misery. They may approach you quite defensively. What would your response be? If you too became defensive or angry, you could be responding to this person's transference, with counter transference possibly from experiences in your own past.

Or imagine someone who saw you as 'the good mummy' and you respond by mothering him this could be your counter transference. To do this may trigger the start of a victim/rescuer relationship.

Counter transference is when we respond to another persons transference from our own feelings which stems from relationships in our past (either our most recent past or from years ago).

Not all 'dislike' for others is transference, it is important to bear in mind that our memory can also be a tool to help us to avoid repeating past mistakes, and attracting relationships that are not so good for us. It may at times be our gut instinct so it is important to listen to our head and our hearts.

Process this learning for a while. Explore your own transference issues. As uncomfortable as it may feel, it does assist you on your journey of emotional growth.

Introduction to Counselling Skills and Theory

It helps you to be more accepting of others and improves your relationships now and in the future.

Look at the following behaviours and write down your immediate responses:

1. Someone who is hostile towards you.

2. Someone who believes you are a semi divine being

3. Someone who gets angry with you

4. Someone who is going one up (one upmanship)

5. Someone who sits dejectedly in the corner

It's possible that, if you have been honest, your responses are your counter transference. Look at the following examples, were your responses similar?

Someone who is hostile towards you	DEFENSIVE
Someone who believes you are a semi divine being	ARROGANT
Someone who gets angry with you	ANGRY
Someone who is going one up (One upmanship)	RUDE
Someone who sits dejectedly in the corner	RESCUING

Introduction to Counselling Skills and Theory

If you respond with your counter transference you are more likely to be in conflict or difficulties within your relationships. We cannot control other people's transference, but we can be responsible for our own responses once we are aware.

The idea is to respond from the 'here and now,' freely, and not respond from our own past issues. It's important also to be honest. Here are some examples of healthy, here and now responses:

Healthy response

Hostile	I sense your hostility and I am wondering what is going on for you
Semi DivineBeing	I am worried that you see me as something I am not
Anger	I can see you are angry with me can we sit down and talk

In a nutshell the Psychological definition of transference is the experience of feelings to a person, which do not befit that person and which actually apply to another. Essentially, a person in the present is reacted to as though he were a person in the past.

If you are aware of this in a relationship with a client then it is important for you to explore and work with the transference or counter transference either with the client

Introduction to Counselling Skills and Theory

if appropriate by using immediacy skills, in your own therapy or clinical supervision.

> **Thoughts:**
>
> Have you recognised any transference or counter transference in your personal relationships?
>
> Have you been able to use this knowledge and tool to disconnect from your past and relate in the 'here and now'.

Introduction to Counselling Skills and Theory

Chapter 30
Personal Development
Self Esteem

Self esteem is the opinion you have of yourself. You can't touch it, but it effects how you feel. You can't see it, but it's there when you look in the mirror. You can't hear it, but it is there every time you talk about yourself.

Having a high self esteem is not boasting about how great you are. It is more like quietly knowing that you are worth a lot, priceless in fact. It is not about thinking you are perfect – because nobody is – but knowing that you are worthy of being loved and accepted.

Nor is self esteem like a new dress or shirt that you'd love to have, but don't have. Everyone needs to have self esteem.

A good self esteem is important. It helps you to hold your head up high and feel proud of yourself. It gives you the

Introduction to Counselling Skills and Theory

courage to try new things and the power to believe in yourself. It empowers you to make changes in your life, reach goals and respect yourself.

So start raising your self esteem today………. by:

Loving and accepting yourself, if you can do this then you can accept that you are human and subsequently accept that to make mistakes is human.

Celebrating your strengths and achievements, forgiving yourself for your mistakes and not dwelling on your weaknesses, every human being has them.

Change the way that you talk to yourself and stop putting yourself down. Do not judge yourself against unreasonable expectations and stop beating yourself up for your weaknesses.

I would now like to share with you one of my favourite tools that I use with people with a low self esteem. It also keeps my self esteem high.

Take a piece of A4 paper and put a line down the middle. On the left hand side of the paper I would like you to write down the name of five significant people in your life that you really admire. (It does not matter if they are still with us or not).

This may take some time.

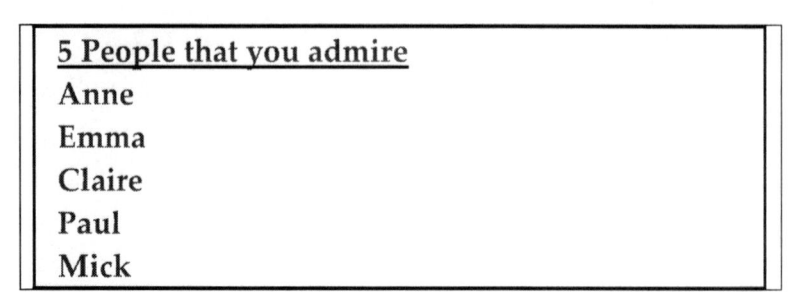

Introduction to Counselling Skills and Theory

5 People that you admire
Anne
Emma
Claire
Paul
Mick

Now write down on the right hand side all the things that you admire about them. Try to choose three different qualities for each person.

5 people that you admire	What you admire about them
Anne	Caring, straightforward, brave
Emma	Good sense of humour, empathic, non-judgemental
Claire	Kind, helpful, chatty
Paul	Loyal, fun, spirited
Mick	Honest, laid back, calm

Tear the paper in half and put the left part in the bin, (the people you admire).

Write at the top of the page "I AM........." Now read out aloud all the things that you are.

"It is not possible to recognize these qualities in others unless you have them yourself!!!"

Introduction to Counselling Skills and Theory

So yes all those qualities that you have written down, is you , as it's not possible to recognise qualities in others unless you have them yourself. How neat is that?

Now what I would like you to do before you go any further. I would like you to turn that piece of paper about yourself into a poster, and I would also like you to make some little cards with your qualities on.

Now copy those posters around the house and keep your card in your bag or pocket and when you are having a low day. Go read your qualities.

Here's my example:

I AM…………..
Caring
Straight forward
Brave
Good sense of humor
Empathic
Non-judgmental
Kind
Helpful
Chatty

Introduction to Counselling Skills and Theory

> Loyal
> Fun
> Spirited
> Honest
> Laid-back
> Calm

If I had asked you to write down **15** positives about yourself, would you have been able to do that? People with a low self esteem would struggle to name three.

Read your qualities out loud. Remind yourself. Be compassionate to yourself.

Often we can be extremely compassionate towards others and yet extremely harsh towards ourselves. I often find myself asking clients "If this was a friend would you be this harsh on them" and they very rarely would, so why themselves?

Try using some compassion to change your mind, about your negative thoughts and feelings about yourself.

Introduction to Counselling Skills and Theory

Chapter 31

Different approaches to counselling

Apart from the structure or frame work of counselling there are also theoretical approaches to it.

These approaches have evolved from three principal schools or orientations.

The Psychodynamic Approach: - Origins in Freudian theory. This model stresses the importance of childhood experience. - Establishes links between past and present by drawing parallels between what happened in childhood and what is currently happening in the adult in the here and now.

Behavioural Approach: - This orientation focuses on observable behaviour It stems from the work of many psychologists. Experiments were done on animals at the beginning of the century to validate their theories.

Introduction to Counselling Skills and Theory

The theory is that people's problems stem from learned behaviours which are problematic. For example, phobias or obsessions. The objective of this approach is to help the client to unlearn these patterns through a process of behaviour modification

Humanistic Approach: - This approach gives power back to the client and assumes that the client themselves has intuitive knowledge of what it is that they need and want. Their problems are seen as unique to them.

The objective of this approach is to facilitate the client toward self actualization, integration, and wholeness. Counsellors these days tend to take on a more eclectic approach.

An eclectic counsellor will draw upon multiple theories to gain insight into phenomena. The belief is that many factors influence human behaviour, therefore it is important to utilise a number of theoretical models.

This means that they will integrate their models of learning to meet the clients learning style, characteristic and/or presenting problem. There is a common belief amongst the profession that 'one model does not fit all.' This applies to even the evidence based models too. Our clients are unique, they are different therefore it makes sense that they are not all going to 'suit' the same model of therapy.

Introduction to Counselling Skills and Theory

However, critics will say that this way of working is inconsistent.

In the next chapters I will briefly discuss four theoretical models:

- ✓ Transactional Analysis,
- ✓ Cognitive Behavioural Therapy,
- ✓ Person Centred
- ✓ Psychodynamic.

I will discuss the main concepts of these models. This may lead you to further reading on one of the models if it appeals to you, or indeed all of them. The Diploma course will follow one particular model of training for two to four years, although more and more training providers now are running integrative courses to enable you to work in an eclectic way.

> **Thoughts:**
>
> What are your thoughts?
>
> What model of theory appeals to you?

Introduction to Counselling Skills and Theory

Chapter 32

Cognitive Behavioral Therapy

CBT is a type of talking therapy. The founder was Aaron Beck who expanded on the work done by Behaviour therapist Albert Ellis.

It combines cognitive therapy and behavioural therapy. It focuses on how you 'think' about the things going on in your life. It looks predominantly at the cognitive process (thoughts, images, beliefs and attitudes) and how this impacts on the way that you behave and deal with emotional problems.

CBT theorists would say that most of the 'bad feelings' we have come from negative thoughts or distortions, and that through identifying the lie behind the thought we can change the way we feel.

The belief is that if we change:

Introduction to Counselling Skills and Theory

- Negative patterns

- Thinking

- Beliefs

- Behaviour

Then we can change the way that we feel

CBT suggests:

- That it is not events that upset you but the meanings that you give to them.

- Your thoughts can block you from seeing things that do not fit with what you believe is true.

- You may hold on to these thoughts and not learn anything new.

CBT tends to be:

- Short term – 6 weeks to 6 months

- Once a week for one hour

It is currently the evidence based model for substance misuse, depression, anxiety and phobias, OCD and PTSD. It can also help with:

Introduction to Counselling Skills and Theory

- Anger management

- Panic attacks

- Chronic fatigue syndrome

- Chronic pain

- Eating disorders

- General health problems

- Habits

- Mood swings

- Relationship problems

Clinical trials have shown that CBT can reduce symptoms of many emotional disorders. Nice (The National Institute for Clinical Excellence) recommended CBT for the NHS, hence why we now have the IAPT Service.

A CBT therapist will:

- Explore the problems

- Develop a plan for attacking them

- Help you to learn a new set of principles

Introduction to Counselling Skills and Theory

- Help you to change your thoughts to more realistic thoughts that will in turn change your feeling and your behavior

S/he will:

- Focus on the present

- In longer term therapy will explore how the present impacts on the now but does not stay on the past nor do any work in the past

- Set homework tasks

- Set goals

There is a structure to CBT therapy and it is a joint discussion. It is a directive therapy. "Giving the client the tools to build their own house rather than leaving them to find their own"

The therapist will help the client to see how their thoughts activate their feelings, physical symptoms and subsequently their behavior. They will then give the client tools to help them to change their thoughts to a more positive one, which in turn will change the way that they feel emotionally and physically and contribute towards more healthy behavior. The model on the next page looks at a client with the belief that he is worthless

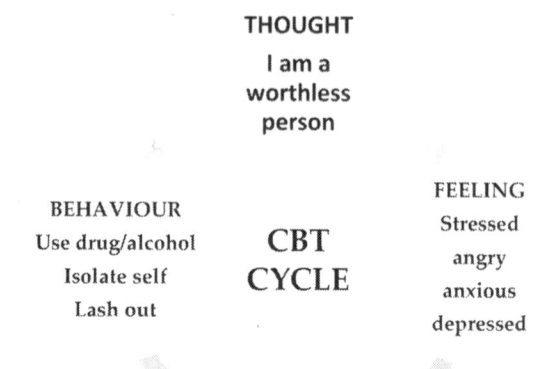

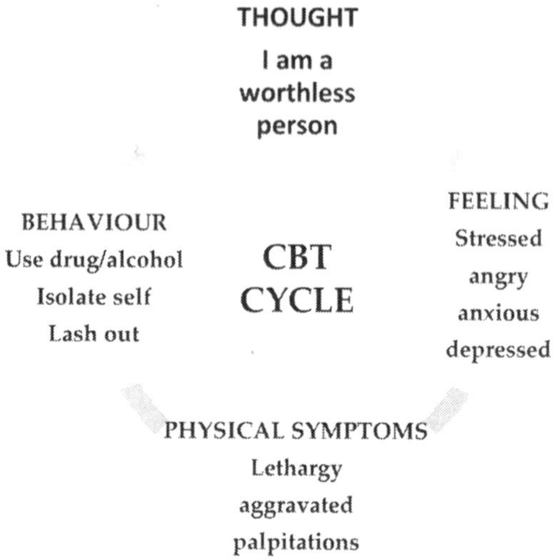

Introduction to Counselling Skills and Theory

THOUGHT
I am a worthless person

BEHAVIOUR
Use drug/alcohol
Isolate self
Lash out

CBT CYCLE

FEELING
Stressed
angry
anxious
depressed

PHYSICAL SYMPTOMS
Lethargy
aggravated
palpitations

The therapist will draw this cycle out with the client and then explore exit points on the diagram.

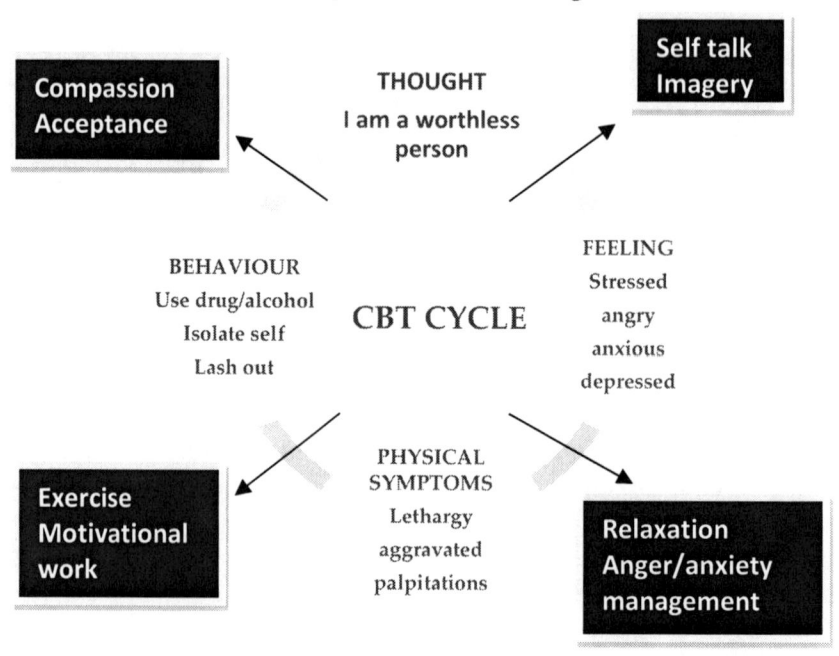

Compassion Acceptance

THOUGHT
I am a worthless person

Self talk Imagery

BEHAVIOUR
Use drug/alcohol
Isolate self
Lash out

CBT CYCLE

FEELING
Stressed
angry
anxious
depressed

Exercise Motivational work

PHYSICAL SYMPTOMS
Lethargy
aggravated
palpitations

Relaxation Anger/anxiety management

Introduction to Counselling Skills and Theory

The black boxes on the previous page on the CBT cycle are tools that can be used to help the client to see that there thought is not the truth. I will briefly explain what these tools are:

Self Talk: Is teaching the client to reality test their thoughts with their internal voice in their head.

Imagery: Is any words that create a picture in your head. It is also a term used to refer to any creation or re-creation of any experience in the mind. It is a cognitive process employed by most people.

One of my favorite ways of using imagery is as follows:

To use imagery for challenging your negative thoughts, firstly I need you to think about someone famous, this may be an actress, politician, sports personality or comedian that you really do not like, that you think talks a lot of rubbish (bear in mind this will be your perception).

If this person entered the room you would walk out, because nothing s/he said would be interesting, honest or make any sense.

Let's use mine and bear in mind, I cannot use real celebrities names in this book for obvious reasons, so I will use a pseudo name

Introduction to Counselling Skills and Theory

JOHN CARNEY

Now I'd like you to think of someone, who you admire and feel, talks a lot of sense. Think of someone who you could sit and listen to for hours.

SHARON OSWELL

<u>Now choose your own.</u>

The first person (*in my example John Carney*) is your negative thoughts, your critical self, you internal bully. The second person (*in my example Sharon Oswell*) is your positive thoughts, your nurturing self, the self that will challenge bullies, and challenge the things that are not the truth. Now think about one of your negative thoughts, again I will use one of my own:

Linda you are getting old and wrinkly, there is no point doing anything now at your age.

Now say to yourself "NO this is your bullying person (John Carney) speaking, before I believe this I will ask what your nurturing person (Sharon Oswell) thinks.

In my example Sharon says:

Linda, everyone gets older but you look pretty good for your age, there is plenty of life in you yet, plenty of opportunities and plenty of skills to put to good use.

Introduction to Counselling Skills and Theory

Which thought should I listen to?

Which thought is the truth?

If I listened to 'John Carney' I would feel low, lethargic, and angry, disappointed and may even become depressed.

If I listen to Sharon then I will feel good, energised, motivated and calm. It is quite clear which of these statements are the truth and yet most of us choose to listen to the lie, most of us will not challenge the lie.

Relaxation: Is teaching the client some relaxation or meditation techniques.

Anger/Anxiety Management: Teaching the client how to manage their anger or anxiety

By the time the client gets to the physical symptoms triggered by their negative thought, the above tools may not be powerful enough, so a CBT therapist might teach the client more active tools such as:

- **Exercise**

- **More motivational tools**

It is just as important to prepare the client in the event that s/he has acted out on their thoughts and feelings and

Introduction to Counselling Skills and Theory

behaved unhealthily. The CBT therapist may at this point teach the client:

- **Compassion:** Maybe to write a compassionate letter to themselves.

- **Acceptance:** To teach the client to be more acceptance of self, warts and all.

If you could help the client to change that thought then his/her cycle might look like this:

THOUGHT
I have lots of fine qualities
I am a good person

BEHAVIOUR
Friendly
Sociable
Smiley/Open

cbt cycle

FEELINGS
Happy
Positive
Motivated

PHYSICAL SYMPTOMS
Energetic
Calm
Relaxed

Introduction to Counselling Skills and Theory

Thoughts:

Try using this model on your own negative thoughts.

Introduction to Counselling Skills and Theory

Chapter 33
Person Centred Therapy

Person Centred Therapy, also known as Client centred therapy or Rogerian Psychotherapy, was developed by the humanist Carl Rogers in the 1940's and 1950's.

It is one of the most widely used models in mental health and psychotherapy.

The basic elements of Rogerian therapy involve showing clients the core conditions which we have discussed in a previous chapter. Based on these elements the therapist creates a supportive, non judgemental environment in which the client is encouraged to reach their full potential.

PCT is used to help a person achieve personal growth and/or come to terms with a specific event or problem. It is based on the principal of talking therapy and unlike cognitive behavioural therapy it is a non directive approach.

Introduction to Counselling Skills and Theory

The therapist encourages the client to express their feelings and does not suggest how the person might wish to change, but by listening and then mirroring back what the client reveals to them, helps them to explore and understand their feelings for themselves. The client is then able to decide what kind of changes they would like to make and can achieve personal growth.

Although this technique has been criticized by some for its lack of structure and set method, it has proves to be a hugely effective and popular treatment.

Rogers devised six conditions of change for a client to be able to find their own solution to their own problem. These are:

1. **Therapist-Client Psychological Contact.**

   - A relationship between client and therapist must exist.

   - In must be a relationship in which each person's perception of the other is important.

2. **Client incongruence or vulnerability.**

   - The incongruence exists between the clients experience and awareness.

Introduction to Counselling Skills and Theory

- Furthermore, the client is vulnerable to anxiety which motivates them to stay in the relationship.

3. **Therapist congruence and genuineness**

    - The therapist is congruent within the therapeutic relationship.

    - The therapist is deeply his or herself – they are not 'acting' – and they are drawing on their own experiences (self disclosure) to facilitate the relationship.

4. **Therapist unconditional positive regard**

    - The therapist accepts the client unconditionally, without judgement, disapproval or approval.

    - His facilitates increased self regard in the client, as they can begin to become aware of experiences in which their view of self worth was distorted by others.

5. **Therapist empathic understanding**

    - The therapist experiences an empathic understanding of the client's frame of reference.

Introduction to Counselling Skills and Theory

- Accurate empathy on the part of the therapist helps the client believe the therapists unconditional love for them.

6. **Client Perception:**

- That the client perceives, to at least a minimal degree, the therapist's UPR and empathic understanding.

Rogers believed that this was all that was needed to facilitate a client's growth. There was no time limit on this therapy. It was recognised that every client was different in how and when they reached their solution to their own problem. Therefore this is harder to facilitate in time limited therapy.

Conditions of worth.

Amongst other theories of Rogers, he believed that we all have conditions of worth.

A condition of worth is a value that is put on us at a very early age.

For example:

"A child may feel that he is loved when he is told that he is being 'a good boy,' but not when he has misbehaved. This creates condition of worth, where the child feels that

Introduction to Counselling Skills and Theory

he becomes worthy of love only when his actions are consistent with what is expected of him."

The positive regard of others should not have strings attached but often does. Over time, this may result in conditional self regard, where we are only worth something if we meet the conditions that others have imposed on us.

For example:

"I failed my exams, so I am useless"

"I need to be rich to be happy"

These conditions of worth can have a huge affect on our thoughts, feelings and behaviour and a adverse affect on our relationships and our life.

> **Thoughts:**
>
> Explore what your own conditions of worth might be.
>
> Are they helpful or unhelpful?

Introduction to Counselling Skills and Theory

Chapter 34
Transactional analysis

Transactional analysis is a theory of personality and systematic psychotherapy for personal growth and personal change. The founder of T.A is Eric Berne.

As a theory of personality it describes how people are structured psychologically. It uses what is its best known model. "The ego state model" to do this:

What Eric Berne believes is that we all have three states, those states he calls 'ego sates.' He states that we slip in and out of these states repeatedly all through our daily lives. He discusses how it depends on what state that you are in on how your day/life pans out. If we are in the right ego state at the right time then our thoughts, feelings, behaviour and indeed lives will be healthier.

His ego states have a similarity to Freuds 'Super ego, ego and ID.

Introduction to Counselling Skills and Theory

Eric Berne's Ego State Model

P

A

C

This is what Eric Berne called his PAC Model/Ego state Model.

The P represents Parent. The A is Adult and the C is Child. He believes that we move from one state to another several times a day in our transactions with others.

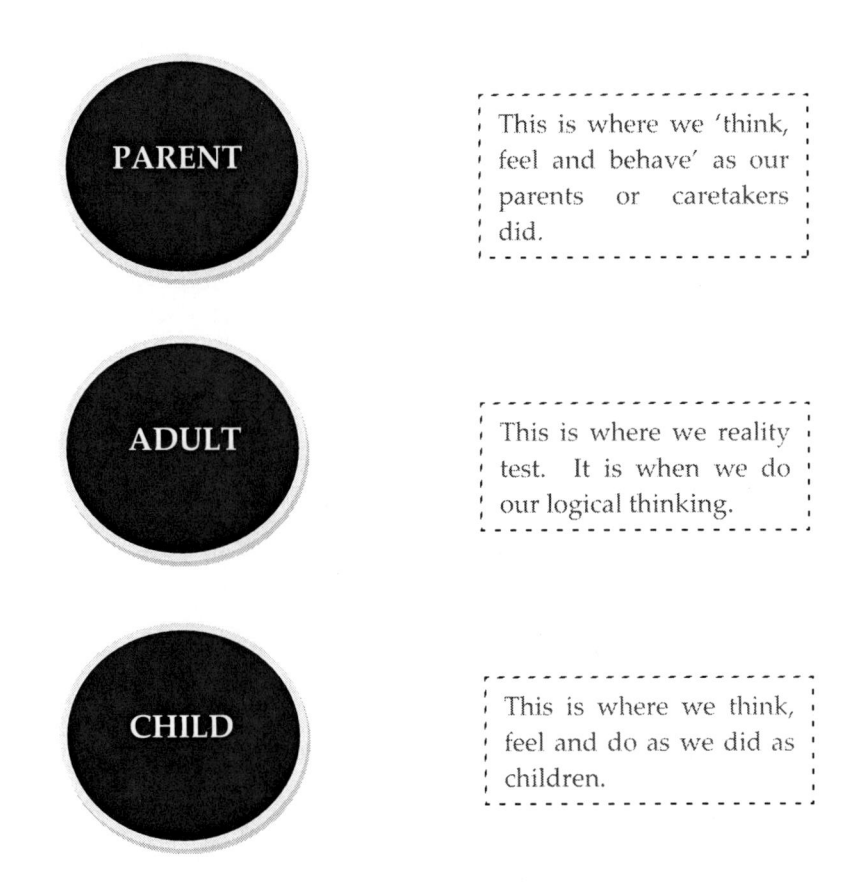

Introduction to Counselling Skills and Theory

PARENT — This is where we 'think, feel and behave' as our parents or caretakers did.

ADULT — This is where we reality test. It is when we do our logical thinking.

CHILD — This is where we think, feel and do as we did as children.

Transactional analysis informs us that our **'parent'** ego state is where we store our parental values and opinions.

We may express prejudice, critical and nurturing behaviour towards others from this state. Berne informs us that our parental messages from our childhood continue to influence our inner child.

He calls it 'the should ego state.'

Introduction to Counselling Skills and Theory

Our **'adult'** ego state is not related to a person's age. It is orientated toward current reality and the objective gathering of information. When you are in this state you are organised, adaptable and intelligent. You are able to test reality and estimate probabilities.

It is known to 'compute dispassionately.'

The **'child'** ego state has all the impulses that come naturally to an infant. This state holds all our early experiences and the positions that we took about ourselves and others. When in the state we act out all our 'childhood' behaviours. It holds feelings of happiness, anxiety, fear, withdrawal etc.

If is when you are 'feeling like you did when you were a child.'

Remember we use all these ego states to communicate with others (outwardly). We also use them inwardly, we have all experienced our internal parent tapes in our head.

So in a nutshell if we have very critical messages in our parent ego state we will be very critical of others and also very critical of ourselves. Healthier people have a strong nurturing **'parent'** ego state as they are able to nurture others and nurture self.

Introduction to Counselling Skills and Theory

We have the ability in therapy or self help using this model to change our external and internal critical parent. We are able to do this using our **'adult'** ego state. The **'adult'** ego state gives a person a measure of objectivity. It can evaluate what is going on in our **'parent'** and **'child'** programming and decide what is all right and what needs to be changed.

We can use our **'adult'** to reason, evaluate stimuli, to gather information for future reference. It enables a person to use data to make decisions and implement those decisions.

Transactional Analysis and interpersonal relationships.

Bear in mind that if we have three ego states that we relate from then so does everyone else on this earth. While we are communicating and jumping between ego states so are the people we communicate with. Is it any wonder that we sometimes struggle to understand each other.

The difficulty in interpersonal relationships comes from being in the 'wrong' ego state at the 'wrong' time. The safest bet would be to stay in **'adult'** at all times, but how boring would that be?

The truth is that it is healthy to be in all your ego states, once you learn about them and learn which to be in at the right time. To do this you need to become ego state

Introduction to Counselling Skills and Theory

aware, and to reflect on when things go wrong in your interpersonal relationships on what ego state you were in at the time.

Interpersonal relationships
Complimentary Transaction

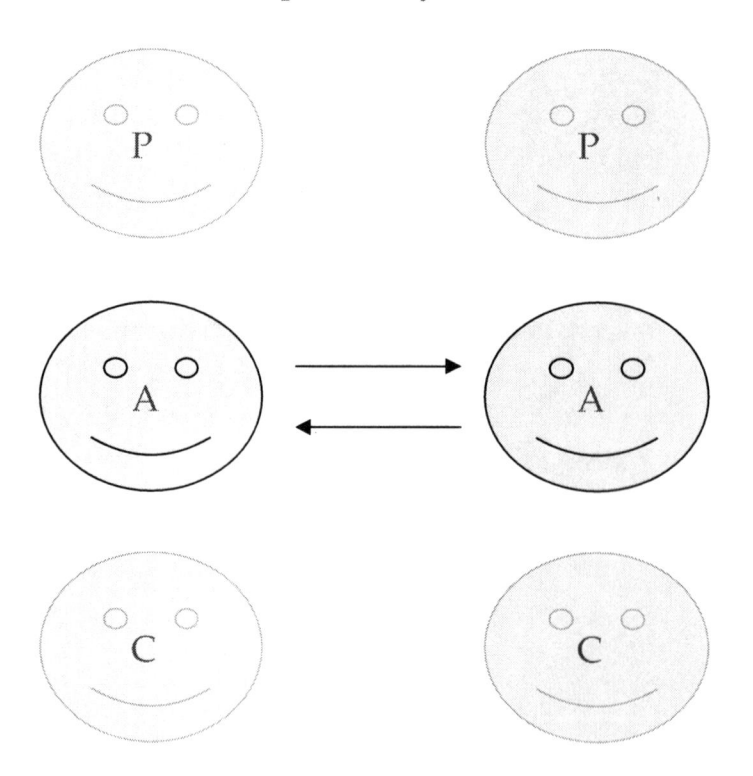

In communications between two or more people there is various stimuli and responses. These form the core of our transactions. The above is **adult** to **adult**. This is known as complimentary communication. A complimentary transaction is when a transaction gets the expected response from a specific ego state in the other person.

Introduction to Counselling Skills and Theory

For example:

"Do you know where the remote control is?

"Yes it is on the coffee table"

Ulterior Transaction

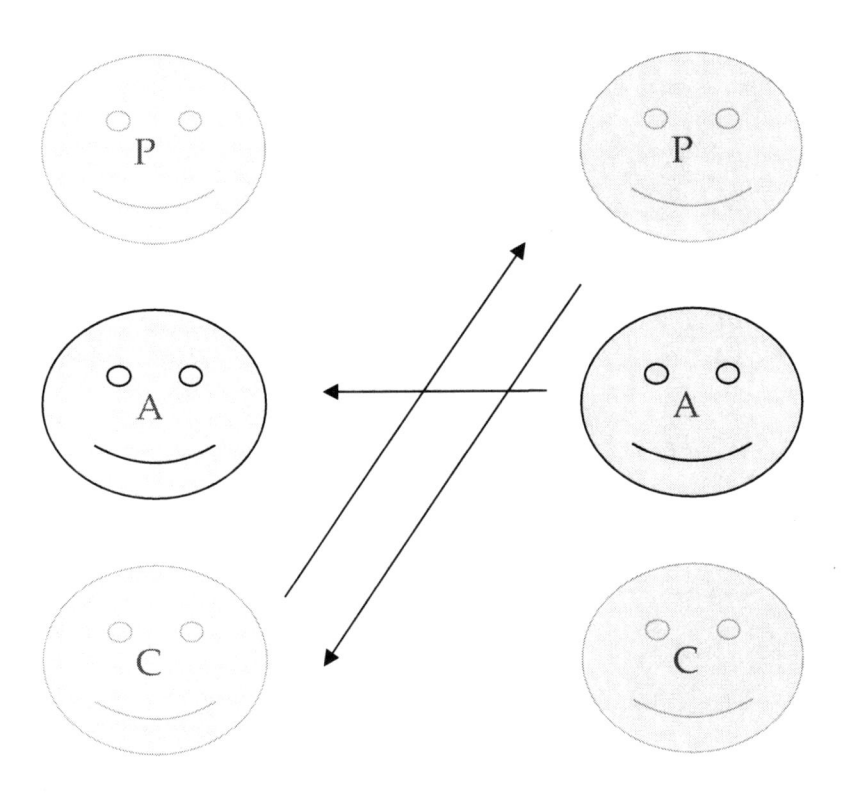

This is when a transaction has a hidden message and it hooks the ego state the hidden message was aiming for not the one the original message was aimed at.

Introduction to Counselling Skills and Theory

For example:

"Do you know where the remote control is?"

"I can't find anything when I need it" (Looks sad and helpless)

"Don't worry I will find it for you" (Gives affectionate look)

It is where the ulterior message is more important to the sender than the overt message.

Crossed Transactions

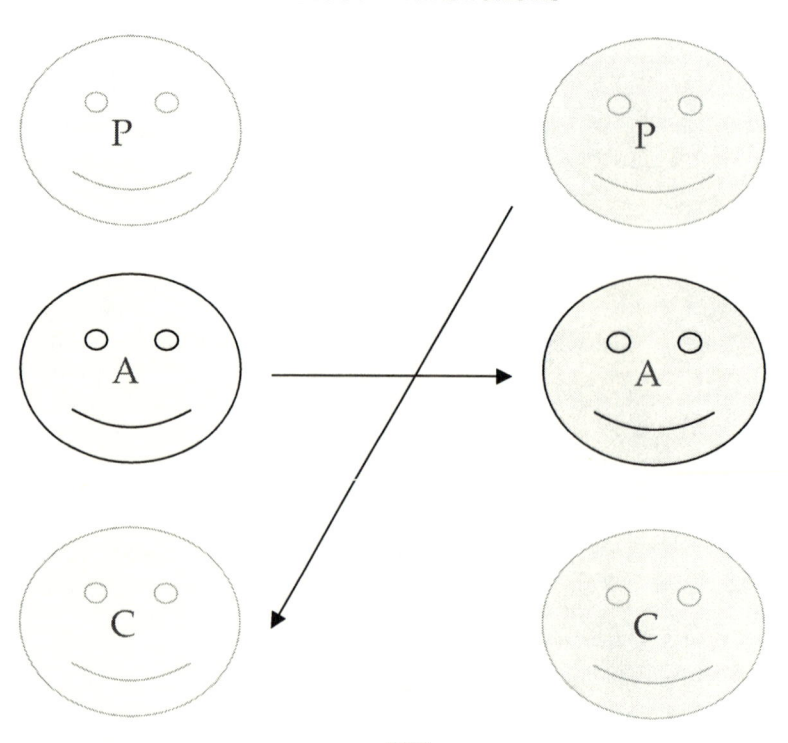

Introduction to Counselling Skills and Theory

A crossed transaction gets an unexpected response from a unexpected ego state in the other person.

These transactions are a frequent source of resentment between people.

For example:

"Do you know where the remote is?"

"It's right where you left it, can't you remember anything!"

This is all of course all out of our conscious awareness, until now that is. To reiterate, we all have three different ego states programmed with different behaviour, having this awareness gives you more choices in your communication pattern.

> **Thoughts:**
>
> Become aware of when you are coming from your **adult, parent** and **child** in your communication with others.
>
> Think of a time when you were in conflict with someone, what ego state were you in?

Introduction to Counselling Skills and Theory

Chapter 35
Personal Development
Ego- gram

For your personal development I am going to invite you to do your own ego gram. To do this I need to explain a little more about about the **'parent'** and the **'child'** ego state, firstly the **'parent:'**

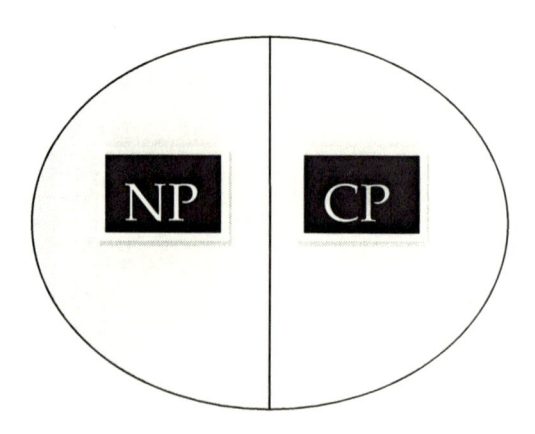

Introduction to Counselling Skills and Theory

Our **'parent'** ego state has two parts to it. A **'critical parent'** and a **'nurturing parent,'** this is both internal and external, and we can operate from either.

Now for the **'child'** ego state.

This does not mean behaving childishly but is concerned with behaviour and feelings as they were experienced in childhood

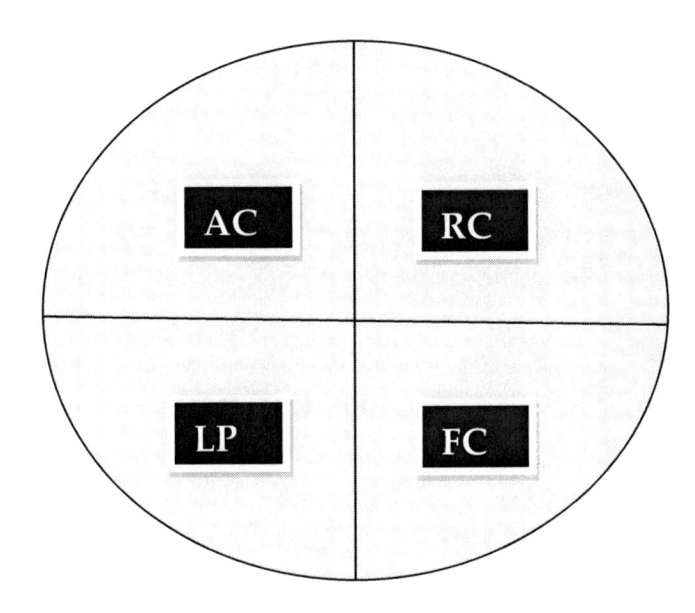

Our **'child'** ego state has four parts as follows:

- AC = Adapted Child
- RC = Rebellious Child
- LP = Little Professor
- FC = Free Child

Introduction to Counselling Skills and Theory

Like the **'parent,'** we can operate from any one of those four states. This is what each of them mean.

Adapted Child: This is the child that wants to be a hairdresser but becomes a doctor because our parents want us 'to be.' When we are older, we move into Adapted Child when we demonstrate that we know how to behave. By now much of this is automatic and we are barely conscious of it.

Rebellious Child: This is the part of us that rebels against what is expected of us.

Little Professor: This is the curious part of us, the part that wants to explore, analyses and questions. This is the 'little know it all' within us.

Free Child: Is the natural child, it is the part of us that is spontaneous, fun loving and inhibited. We are born free with no prejudices or conditions placed on us.

Now that you have a further understanding of the PAC model you can start to do your ego gram. On the following page you will see a list of words. You will need to tick the words that you use internally or externally on a regular basis.

Don't think too hard, if you have to think you probably don't use it. Be spontaneous and take a maximum of 10 minutes to do this.

Introduction to Counselling Skills and Theory

1.	2.	3.	4.
Never	Very good	Correct	Wow
Should	Nice	How	Sensual
You ought	Look after	Factual	I want
You must	Splendid	Why	Sexy
Right	Tender	Results	Bubbly
Always	Poor thing	Practical	Scared
It's wrong	Don't worry	Alternative	I love it
Ridiculous	Let me	Detached	Lively
Do this	Be careful	Objective	Mine
Don't	Supporting	Serious	Secret
Critical	Encouraging	Capable	Free
Condescending	Comforting	Confident	Excited
Sneering	Sympathetic	Even	Loud
Bossy	Concerned	Calm	Giggling
Disgusted	Protective	Unemotional	Angry
Hard	Accepting	Thoughtful	Inhibited
Controlling	Smiling	Alert	Energetic
Frowning	M/Paternal	Honest	Spontaneous
Rigid	Consoling	Interested	Flirtatious
Condemning	Understanding	Open mind	Eager
Judgmental	Caring	Rational	Emotional
Moralistic	Giving	Balanced	Fun loving
Authorization	Nurturing	Logical	Changeable
Principals	Helpful	Sober	Laughing
Total ticks	Total ticks	Total ticks	Total Ticks

Introduction to Counselling Skills and Theory

5.	6.	7.
Can't	Let's try	Won't
Wish	How about?	Why should I
Try	I have an idea	It's unfair
Hope	Clever	Resentful
Please	Discovery	Sullen
Sorry	Ingenious	Defiant
Thank you	Artistic	Pouting
I ought	Organizing	Vengeful
Excuse me	Curious	Rebellious
After you	Creative	Bolshy
Whining	Questioning	Contrary
Submissive	Intent	Make me
Quiet	Winking	Obstinate
Placating	Devious	Abrupt
Apologetic	Enquiring	Stroppy
Pleasing	Persuasive	Sceptical
Sad	Insinuating	Stubborn
Passive	Manipulative	Independent
Worried	Problem-solving	Resistant
Agreeing	Inventive	Unhelpful
Guilty	Resourceful	Argues
Cautious	Imaginative	NO!
Anxious	Smart	Anarchic
Weak		Bog off
Total ticks _____	Total ticks _____	Total ticks _____

Introduction to Counselling Skills and Theory

Okay, now you can do your ego gram.

1. Is your Critical Parent
2. Is your Nurturing Parent
3. Is your Adult
4. Is your Free Child
5. Is your Adapted Child
6. Is your Little Professor
7. Is your Rebellious Child

Transfer your scores on to a graph as the following example:

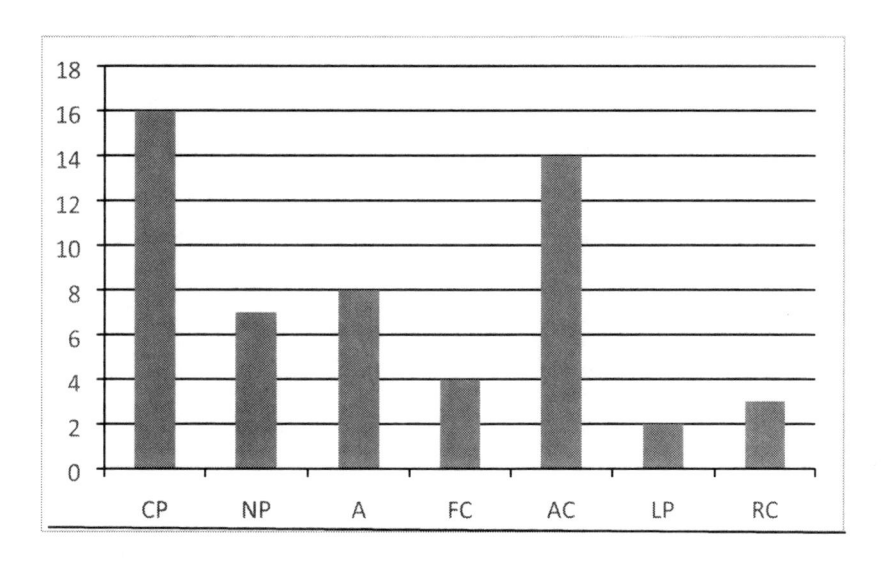

Category	Score
CP	16
NP	7
A	8
FC	4
AC	14
LP	2
RC	3

This then becomes your 'ego-gram'.

This person has a high critical parent and adapted child. His rebellious child is very low. This tells me that this

Introduction to Counselling Skills and Theory

person may be a people pleaser that very rarely says "No". S/he does not nurture themselves enough and is not very spontaneous.

If you look at your ego gram it helps you to identify where you may want to make changes and explore ways of making that change.

Thoughts:

What did you learn from your ego-gram?

Did you identify any changes you might want to make?

Introduction to Counselling Skills and Theory

Chapter 36

The Psychodynamic Approach

Psychodynamic therapy, also known as insight-oriented therapy, focuses on unconscious processes as they are manifested in a person's present behaviour.

The goals of psychodynamic therapy are a client's self-awareness and understanding of the influence of the past on present behaviour.

In its brief form, a psychodynamic approach enables the client to examine unresolved conflicts and symptoms that arise from past dysfunctional relationships and manifest themselves in mental health symptoms and the need and desire to abuse substances.

It was Sigmund Freud whom first developed psychoanalysis therapy. His most important contribution to psychology was the concept of the 'unconscious mind'

Introduction to Counselling Skills and Theory

and how this played an important role in how a person behaved.

"If you get caught speeding several times, how might you now behave?"

"If you fell off a ladder several times, how might you now behave?"

Therefore if you experienced several real or imagined rejections, abandonments or abuse, how might you now behave?

Freud and more modern day psychoanalysts believe that any individual's behaviour is the direct result of all prior experience, particularly our experiences from childhood.

He believed that our first experiences formed solid foundations on which the developing child would structure the rest of his life.

In other words the adult personality was directly formed in childhood.

If the child experiences were happy and balanced then the child could develop into a normal well balanced and adjusted adult.

Freud believed that we have three conscious states:

Introduction to Counselling Skills and Theory

The Conscious

The Sub conscious

The Unconscious

The conscious is our everyday awareness – we are sitting in our conscious state now and we are reading this line of text on the power point listening to the tutor.

The sub conscious is the things that we have to think about if asked i.e. a telephone number, our first ever address, our child's date of birth etc. They lie dormant until needed.

The unconscious is the unknown. This is the stuff that is not in our conscious awareness. Freud would say it is the contents of our unconscious that comes out in our dreams.

The unconscious is the stuff that we are not aware of and that therapy may bring us to awareness of in order for us to change the unhealthy thoughts, feelings and behaviours that we have carried over from childhood.

Freud also describes us as having three parts of the psychic apparatus.

The id
The super-ego

Introduction to Counselling Skills and Theory

The ego

According to this model of the psyche, he describes:

- The **id** as the set of uncoordinated instinctual trends

- The **super-ego** plays the critical and moralising role

- The **ego** is the organised, realistic part that mediates between the desires of the **id** and the **super ego.**

And

- The **Super-ego** can stop you from doing certain things that your **id** may want you to do.

You may now be able to see the similarity between Freud's super ego, ego and ID and Berne's Parent, Adult and Child.

Parent (Super ego)

Adult (Ego)

Child (Id)

The super ego (parent) deals with the task of balancing demands. This is where we store all our negative and

Introduction to Counselling Skills and Theory

positive parental messages. This is the part that when our inner child is hungry and there is no food that will stop us from stealing it, or not whichever may be the case.

The id (Child) this is the part that drives our gratifications of basic human needs i.e. air, water, food, warmth, love, shelter, sex etc. This is the part that sulks if our needs are not met, slams doors if we are angry, fights for those needs to be met.

The ego (Adult) this is the part of us that reality tests, looks for the evidence, will tell us that actually we can get our food in a different way other than stealing, that we can get our basic needs met by asking rather then sulking, or acting out our anger.

It is the conflict between these states that causes a lot of our mental distress.

The well balanced individual is said to be **Ego led**

The neurotic is **Super ego led**

The psychopath is **Id led**

Hence, the basic psychodynamic model focuses on the dynamic interactions between the **id, ego** and **super-ego**, subsequently, attempting to explain or interpret behaviour or mental states in terms of innate emotional forces or processes.

Introduction to Counselling Skills and Theory

Psychodynamic therapists will help you make connections between your past experiences and your present problem.

> They fuck you up your mum and dad;
> They may not mean to but they do.
> They fill you with faults they had
> And add some extra just for you.
>
> But they were fucked up in their turn
> By old style fools in hats and coats
> Who half the time were sloppy-stern
> And half at one another's throats.
>
> Man hands on misery to man
> It deepens like a coastal shelf
> Get out as early as you can
> And don't have any kids yourself.
>
> **Phillip Larkin**

Introduction to Counselling Skills and Theory

Chapter 37
Issues that may be brought to counselling & referrals

People may come to you for help for various different issues and when exploring one issue it may raise another, however people often present with the following:

Stress

- Depression
- Anxiety
- Post trauma
- Bereavement
- Phobias
- Sexual abuse

Introduction to Counselling Skills and Theory

- Relationship difficulties
- Child abuse
- Rape
- Abandonment issues
- Rejection issues
- Substance Misuse
- Gambling or other addictions
- Anger management
- Conflict
- Chaos in lives

For each of those issues it is defining a sub type for example:

Stress could be:

- Work related
- Relationship related
- Exam stress

Introduction to Counselling Skills and Theory

- Trauma related
- Time management related

Depression could be:

- Post natal
- Loss related
- Depressive disorder
- Reactive
- Medically related (thyroid, menopause)
- Trauma related

Anxiety could be:

- Generalised anxiety disorder
- Phobia related
- Medically related
- Trauma related

And all could be either related to historical events or recent events or both.

Introduction to Counselling Skills and Theory

Referrals

There will be times in your counselling career that you will have to refer your client on to a more specialised agency.

There are a number of potential reasons for making referrals. These include:

- The client has another need. (e.g. they want information or advice).

- The counsellor lacks specific skills.

- The client requires a specialist (e.g. there is an apparent mental health problem).

- The counsellor knows the client or whom the client is talking about or relative or friend of beyond the professional basis.

- Irresolvable transference issues.

- The counsellor and client are not establishing a therapeutic relationship for some reason (e.g. the client is reluctant to open up to the counsellor; personality differences).

- The counsellor has difficulty with the issues being discussed because they have some kind of personal

Introduction to Counselling Skills and Theory

meaning or take them outside of their comfort zone.

- No progress is being made.

- The client is partaking in disruptive behaviour that might be harmful to themselves or others.

Referral is not a sign of weakness or lack of skill. It does not mean that you cannot provide a safe and therapeutic environment for the client. <u>However,</u> being aware of possible referral agencies ensures that the client can choose the right option for them.

At the core of making a referral is taking action that is best for the client. The clients' best interests should always be paramount.

The BACP guidelines are:

All routine referrals to colleagues and other services should be discussed with the client in advance and the client's consent obtained both to making the referral and also to disclosing information to accompany the referral. Reasonable care should be taken to ensure that:

- The recipient of the referral is able to provide the required service.

Introduction to Counselling Skills and Theory

- Any confidential information disclosed during the referral process will be adequately protected.

- The referral will be likely to benefit the client.

Prior to accepting a referral the practitioner should give careful consideration to:

- The appropriateness of the referral

- The likelihood that the referral will be beneficial to the client

- The adequacy of the client's consent for the referral.

If the referrer is professionally required to retain overall responsibility for the work with the client, it is considered to be professionally appropriate to provide the referrer with brief progress reports. Such reports should be made in consultation with clients and not normally against their explicit wishes.

Introduction to Counselling Skills and Theory

Chapter 38
Endings

Every end is a new beginning

Endings are in the forefront of a counsellors/helpers mind from the beginning of the therapeutic relationship. We are always working towards an ending.

This is the last piece of change in the helping relationship that the helper might have to facilitate.

The ending may be decided by

- The type of professional relationship you have with them

- Organisational constraints

- The therapy being offered

Introduction to Counselling Skills and Theory

- What the client wants (goals of treatment)

- Treatment plan

- Your own personal requirements
- The contract between yourself and the client

- Service provision

It is always better to discuss ending at the beginning rather than say *"When you feel better"* which is as long as a proverbial piece of string.

It is up to you to remind the client of the agreed ending by saying something like:

"We agreed on 8 sessions and we are on our 7th session. Now that we are here, does it still seem like a good time to finish"

A planned positive ending is necessary in the helping relationship to teach the client that all endings are not always 'bad endings'.

A simple way of ending your relationship is to use the last session to look at:

- Where were you when you first came into treatment

- Where are you now

Introduction to Counselling Skills and Theory

- And what are your plans for the future

Although we do our best to plan for a good ending it is not always possible for the following reasons:

- When the client is forced to end, through job change, lack of money

- When the client just stops coming for no apparent reason

- When the client comes for one session says you have been a great help and that they don't need any more sessions

- When you have to refer the client on

- When the client sees you as no help at all and leaves disgruntled

- When the person that you are helping dies

This can leave you as a helper or counsellor with some uncomfortable feelings. They could include anger, sadness, hurt, relief, disappointment.

You could feel:

- Bereaved

Introduction to Counselling Skills and Theory

- Left or abandoned

- Rejected

- Under-valued

- Used

- Lost and purposeless

This is a time when you may need extra support from peers, supervisor or maybe therapy.

Beginnings and endings have a lot in common: they are times of transition, uncertainty, sometimes chaos. They evoke strong emotions: anxiety, rejection, curiosity, excitement, anticipation, fear, sometimes anger and loss.

Above all, the way we have experienced beginnings and endings earlier in our lives will profoundly influence the way we anticipate and experience endings later in our lives too.

But, we can change! We can try and experience a new way of facing endings, whether it is an ending in our control or out of our control it is important to try to be positive about the ending.

Imagine you are standing on the edge of a cliff, on the opposite side is another cliff, it is a cliff that might be

Introduction to Counselling Skills and Theory

where you always wanted to be, it might be a nicer cliff. It is a cliff that you are not familiar with.

You can stand looking at this cliff, fight and kick to avoid this cliff _or_ you can step into the unknown and experience that new beginning.

Thoughts:

Explore the endings in your own life.

How comfortable are you with endings?

This is indeed the ending of our relationship, the journey that we have had through this book. I will leave you with the following poem.

> "I do my thing and you do yours.
> I am not in this world to live up to your expectations, and you are not in this world to live up to mine.
> You are you and I am I, and if by chance we find each other, then it is beautiful.
> If not, it can't be helped."

–Frederick Perls, founder of Gestalt therapy

Introduction to Counselling Skills and Theory

Thank you

Thank you for buying and reading this book. I hope it has helped you with your studies and your own personal growth. I hope to do another edition to support you through your Diploma, but for now I am going to enjoy the Spring, my favourite season, and do some 'taking care of me,' which is another skill you will need to acquire once you start working with 'real' clients.

At some stages of counselling training it can be very emotionally draining. This is because as well as studying the theory, working with your peers in skills practice, you are also working on yourself. This is more than what students will have to contend with on any other academic courses.

It may be a journey and a half. I can't say that it won't be painful at times. But what I can say is that at the end of your journey you will be a changed person and for the better.

> Introduction to Counselling Skills and Theory

Keep going as Cheryl Cole said in the L'oriel advertisements *"Because you are worth it."*

Most importantly

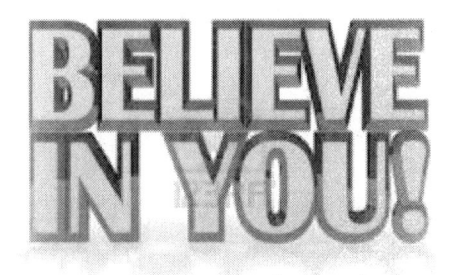

BELIEVE IN YOU!

Introduction to Counselling Skills and Theory

Self help books by Linda Mather.

This is a self help book for everyone's emotional growth. It explores the masks we develop through our lives, how we get them, why and how to get rid of them to facilitate healthy relationships, healthy lifestyle and see the world through fresh eyes.

This is a self help book for people who are suffering with depression. It explores the causes of depression and includes tools to help people to manage their depression.

Introduction to Counselling Skills and Theory

I Shall Be Clean
Self help book for substance misuse
Linda Mather

This is a self help book and a reference book for people who are suffering with addiction and for those working in addiction. It includes several tools to facilitate recovery.

Teenagers Are From Pluto
Ten Tips for Parents of Teenagers
Linda Mather & Michael Mather

This is a tool to help parents through their children's teenage years. It includes tools and humor to help us to manage this difficult stage, and the forever changing relationship.

All available from Amazon or Barnes and Nobel in paperback and e book format.

Introduction to Counselling Skills and Theory

Recommended reading

What's the message?
By Helen Stewart and Simon Carnell

A helpful book for managing challenging behaviour, for parents and professionals

CPSIA information can be obtained at www.ICGtesting.com
Printed in the USA
LVOW11s0037130514

385447LV00005B/487/P